YOU HAVE MASTERED SURVIVAL MODE

IT'S NOW TIME TO LIVE

PASTOR DR. CLAUDINE BENJAMIN

Published by:

Editor: Cleveland O. McLeish (Author C. Orville McLeish)

ISBN: 978-1-965635-34-6 (paperback)

AUTHOR BIO

Pastor Claudine Benjamin is a passionate voice of healing, restoration, and kingdom purpose. A teacher, preacher, counselor, and survivor, she knows firsthand what it means to endure storms, break cycles, and rise from broken places with boldness and grace. For years, Pastor Claudine has been a trusted guide for individuals navigating personal pain, spiritual stagnation, and emotional exhaustion. Her ministry is marked by transparency, prophetic clarity, and a strong mandate to see God's people whole—spirit, soul, and body.

With a heart for the hurting and a message for the masses, she speaks from lived experience and biblical revelation, inspiring countless men and women to not only recover from what broke them, but to live with purpose, power, and passion.

When she's not writing or ministering, Pastor Claudine is empowering others through prayer, mentoring, teaching, and walking in her own assignment of wholeness and truth. She is the author of several life-changing books and devotionals, each one created to ignite faith and launch people out of survival and into freedom.

ACKNOWLEDGMENTS

No journey is ever walked alone. Although much of this book was birthed in private moments of prayer, reflection, and healing, it would not have become what it is without the love, presence, and support of many.

To God—my Sustainer, Healer, and Redeemer. Every word on these pages came through Your grace. Every scar, every testimony, every tear that turned into purpose—I give it back to You in worship. Thank You for never leaving me in survival mode. Thank You for calling me out. Thank You for teaching me how to *live*.

To the Holy Spirit—my Comforter and Counselor. You whispered truth to me when I was weary, reminded me who I was when I forgot, and carried me when my strength gave out. You are my ever-present help, my source of wisdom, and my daily breath.

To my family—thank you for being patient while I poured my heart into this book. Thank you for covering me in prayer, encouraging me to keep writing, and giving me the space to be human, vulnerable, and whole. Your love was a safe place when I needed to heal in peace.

To my friends and inner circle—the ones who checked in, spoke life, sent that perfectly timed word, or simply sat with me through the process. You know who you are. I honor your presence in my life. Thank you for not letting me shrink. Thank you for reminding me who I am.

To every reader—thank you for holding these pages in your hands. You didn't just read this book—you *felt* it. Your journey matters. Your story is sacred. Your decision to heal and live is nothing short of courageous. I pray this book is a mirror, a map, and a mantle for the life you're building.

To the warriors, survivors, overcomers, and visionaries—this message is not just for you, it's *within you.* You have stories to tell. You have wisdom to share. And you have purpose that cannot be destroyed by pain. Thank you for being part of this community of healing, truth, and transformation.

To the editors, designers, formatters, and publishing partners— thank you for stewarding this vision with care. Every detail mattered, and your excellence helped bring these words to life in ways that honored both the message and the mission.

Finally, to the version of me that didn't quit—thank you for staying up late, rising early, praying through the writer's block, and refusing to let fear win. You survived so others could live.

To every name not listed but carried in my heart—this book holds your imprint too.

With deep gratitude,
Pastor Claudine Benjamin

DEDICATION

This book is dedicated to every survivor—To the ones who cried behind closed doors but still showed up.

To the ones who kept pushing even when their hearts were shattered.

To the ones who questioned their worth but dared to keep believing.

To the ones who stayed quiet to keep the peace but are now finding their voice.

To the ones who wore invisible scars and kept loving anyway. This is for you.

To the woman who carried everyone else but didn't know how to rest.

To the man who broke generational curses in silence.

To the dreamer who put their goals on hold just to make it through the day.

To the leader who encouraged everyone but had no one to turn to.

To the mother, father, sister, brother, pastor, friend—you know what it means to keep going when life says "stop."

This is for the *you* who never gave up when giving up felt easier.

You may have walked through the fire, but you did not burn.

You may have lived in the wilderness, but you did not lose your identity.

You may have survived broken, but you're rising whole.

This book is a mirror. A map. A declaration. A reminder that your story isn't over—it's being rewritten with power, purpose, and promise.

To everyone who ever whispered, *"There has to be more to life than this"*—you were right.

This book is for you.

This victory is yours.

This moment is holy.

This life is worth living.

With all my heart, I dedicate this work to your healing, freedom, and future.

TABLE OF CONTENTS

INTRODUCTION

FROM SURVIVAL TO SIGNIFICANCE

There comes a point in every journey where survival is no longer enough. Maybe you've been there—numb but functioning, smiling but silently screaming, showing up but not truly living. You've endured pain, loss, rejection, disappointment, and betrayal. You've faced seasons where breathing was a victory. And through it all, you kept going.

You, my friend, have mastered survival mode.

But now—it's time to live.

This book is for every person who has spent years simply surviving: emotionally, spiritually, mentally, financially, or relationally. Survival mode helped you get through the worst. But if you are reading this, that means you are still here—and being here means you are called to more. You are not meant to camp in survival; you are meant to move forward into significance, joy, healing, and fullness.

John 10:10 says, *"The thief comes only to steal and kill and destroy; I have come that they may have life, and have it to the full." (NIV).* You weren't created to just make it—you were created to live abundantly.

This is your divine permission to step out of survival mode. It's time to thrive, rebuild, reclaim your identity, and walk boldly into the life God has always intended for you.

CHAPTER 1

SURVIVING ISN'T LIVING

Survival mode is a necessary place, but it's not your permanent home. It's the instinctive state your body and mind enter to protect you when life becomes too much. And for a while, it works. It shields you. It numbs you. It carries you through.

But if you stay in survival mode too long, it starts to cost you everything.

You stop dreaming.
You stop planning.
You stop expecting.
You stop *living*.

WHAT SURVIVAL MODE REALLY FEELS LIKE

It's waking up already exhausted. It's scanning every conversation for hidden threats. It's saying "I'm fine" while your heart bleeds behind the scenes. It's functioning out of fear instead of faith. Survival mode makes you a prisoner of the present with no hope for the future.

Somewhere along the way, survival became your lifestyle instead of your lifeline.

But survival was never the end goal—*living* is. And living means engaging with life on purpose, with joy, clarity, and boldness. It means healing what hurt you. It means rebuilding what broke. It means rediscovering who you were before the world wore you down.

GOD NEVER MEANT FOR YOU TO JUST GET BY

The Israelites wandered in the wilderness for 40 years—surviving. They had manna, shelter, and guidance. But it was never the promised land. God sustained them in the wilderness, but He destined them for *Canaan*. He didn't rescue them from Egypt just to wander; He brought them out so they could *enter in*.

You've spent enough time in the wilderness. You've survived Egypt. Now it's time to claim your Canaan.

Deuteronomy 2:3: *"You have been wandering around in this hill country long enough; turn to the north." (NLT).*

There's a turning point. This chapter—this moment—is yours.

SIGNS YOU'RE STILL IN SURVIVAL MODE
- You struggle to trust good things.
- You expect disappointment before it comes.
- You avoid vulnerability.
- You operate in self-protection more than faith.
- You feel stuck, even when things around you change.

Recognize the signs—but don't let them define you.

TODAY IS A NEW CHAPTER

This is not a message of condemnation. It's a declaration of hope. You are more than what you've endured. And the life you desire is not out of reach—it's just on the other side of healing.

Let this chapter be your turning point. Let these words stir something in your spirit. Let God awaken the part of you that dares to believe again.

You have survived.
Now it's time to live.

SCRIPTURES FOR REFLECTION

The thief cometh not, but for to steal, and to kill, and to destroy: I am come that they might have life, and that they might have it more abundantly. —John 10:10

Ye have compassed this mountain long enough: turn you northward. —Deuteronomy 2:3

Behold, I will do a new thing; now it shall spring forth; shall ye not know it? I will even make a way in the wilderness, and rivers in the desert. —Isaiah 43:19

Nay, in all these things we are more than conquerors through him that loved us. —Romans 8:37

Pastor Dr. Claudine Benjamin

I shall not die, but live, and declare the works of the Lord. —Psalm
118:17

CHAPTER 2

WHAT SURVIVAL MODE LOOKS LIKE

S urvival mode is subtle. It's not always screaming or sobbing or shutting the world out.

Sometimes, survival mode is showing up every day, doing what's required, smiling when necessary, and functioning without truly *feeling*. It is the emotional autopilot that helps you avoid crashing— but never helps you soar.

Most people don't even realize they're in it until something forces them to stop.

Some people function in survival mode for weeks. Others live there for years. And the longer you stay, the more normal it feels—even though nothing about it is normal.

You get so used to bracing for the next blow that peace starts to feel suspicious. Rest feels lazy. Joy feels irresponsible. Love feels dangerous.

But God didn't create you to operate in constant defense. You were created to dwell in safety, to move in freedom, and to abide in Him.

THE INTERNAL SIGNS OF SURVIVAL MODE

You might still be in survival mode if:

- You wake up with dread instead of expectation.
- Your emotions stay muted or easily triggered.
- You find yourself disconnected from your own goals and desires.
- You numb out—through food, scrolling, binge-watching, or isolation.
- You go through the motions but feel empty inside.

Internally, survival mode affects your thoughts, self-perception, and faith. You might be praying, but only for emergencies. Reading scripture, but not absorbing it. Showing up to church, but still broken on the inside.

Survival mode doesn't make you weak—it means you're human. But the truth is, God has more for you than just managing pain.

THE EXTERNAL SIGNS OF SURVIVAL MODE

Outwardly, survival mode can still look "successful." You might be:

- Performing well at work, but collapsing emotionally at home.
- Taking care of everyone else while silently falling apart.
- Overcommitting to distract yourself from your own healing.
- Avoiding deep relationships out of fear of being hurt again.

Sometimes, survival looks like busyness. Constant activity. Saying yes to everything just to avoid the silence. Because silence means facing the pain; facing the pain means slowing down long enough to feel again.

But you can't heal what you won't feel.

WHERE DID THIS COME FROM?

Survival mode often originates in trauma—relational betrayal, loss, abuse, church hurt, rejection, abandonment, and failure. Sometimes it stems from childhood. Sometimes from unexpected life storms. Either way, your soul learned how to *protect* itself rather than *trust* again.

The body can't tell the difference between emotional and physical danger—it just reacts. And when your heart is constantly on high alert, your nervous system adapts to stay in a guarded state. You build emotional armor. You stay in control. You avoid risks. You isolate behind strength.

But behind that strength is often a hurting soul crying out for relief.

BIBLICAL EXAMPLES OF SURVIVAL MODE

Let's not forget that even in scripture, many of God's chosen endured survival seasons:

- **Elijah** ran for his life and sat under a broom tree, praying to die (see 1 Kings 19:4). Survival mode.

- **Hagar** fled with her child into the wilderness, convinced they would die—until God met her there (see Genesis 21:15–19).
- **David**, though anointed, spent years on the run, hiding in caves, living like a fugitive. He survived, but God was preparing him to *reign*.

Even **Jesus**, in the Garden of Gethsemane, felt the weight of survival as He cried out in agony—but He didn't stay there. He surrendered. He moved through it. And because of Him, so can we.

WHY YOU CAN'T STAY THERE

Survival is like a shelter in the storm—but what happens when the storm is over, and you're still living in a bunker?

You miss the sunrise.
You miss the harvest.
You miss the joy of the rain ending.

Staying in survival mode too long warps your ability to recognize when you're safe. You sabotage new blessings because they feel unfamiliar. You resist new relationships because you're conditioned to expect pain. You settle for less because the idea of more feels risky.

But here's the truth: **you are not in danger anymore**. And if you are, you won't stay there—because God delivers. Every single time.

THE FIRST STEP OUT OF SURVIVAL MODE

Awareness is the beginning of transformation. You can't change what you don't acknowledge. Today, take a deep breath and ask:

- Am I merely existing or truly living?
- What am I afraid will happen if I stop guarding myself?
- Have I made peace with pain or have I just buried it?

It's time to step out from behind the mask.

It's time to reintroduce yourself—to yourself.

You are not weak because you've been surviving. You are strong because you're still here. But strength now must look like surrender. Healing. Rest.

You've been surviving long enough.

It's time to break free.

SCRIPTURES FOR REFLECTION

But he himself went a day's journey into the wilderness, and came and sat down under a juniper tree: and he requested for himself that he might die; and said, It is enough; now, O Lord, take away my life; for I am not better than my fathers. —1 Kings 19:4

And the water was spent in the bottle, and she cast the child under one of the shrubs. And she went, and sat her down over against him a good way off, as it were a bow shot: for she said, Let me not see the death of the child. And she sat over against him, and lift up her voice, and wept. And God heard the voice of the lad; and the angel of God called to Hagar out of heaven, and said unto her, What aileth thee, Hagar? fear not; for God hath heard the voice of the lad where he is. Arise, lift up the lad, and hold him in thine hand; for I will make him a great nation. And God opened her eyes, and she saw a

---

well of water; and she went, and filled the bottle with water, and gave the lad drink. —Genesis 21:15–19

The Lord is nigh unto them that are of a broken heart; and saveth such as be of a contrite spirit. —Psalm 34:18

Fear thou not; for I am with thee: be not dismayed; for I am thy God: I will strengthen thee; yea, I will help thee; yea, I will uphold thee with the right hand of my righteousness. —Isaiah 41:10

Come unto me, all ye that labour and are heavy laden, and I will give you rest. —Matthew 11:28

DECLARATION

I am not bound by survival mode. I release the need to protect myself from blessings. I declare I am safe in God's presence, healed by His power, and free to live in peace, joy, and fullness. The trauma that tried to break me will not define me. I am alive—and it's time to live.

CHAPTER 3

HOW YOU GOT HERE – TRIGGERS AND TRAUMA

To truly break free from survival mode, we must first understand how we got there.

Survival mode is not random. It is a response. A reaction. A defense mechanism your mind, body, and spirit created to protect you from unbearable emotional and psychological pain. While it served you in a season, it cannot serve you forever.

This chapter will take you on a gentle, yet honest journey of uncovering the "why" behind the walls. You didn't wake up one day and decide to disconnect, distrust, or shut down. It happened little by little, blow by blow, until staying guarded felt safer than being vulnerable.

UNDERSTANDING TRAUMA

Trauma isn't always a catastrophic event. It's often the things we minimize:

- The repeated rejections.

- The unresolved grief.
- The betrayal by someone we trusted.
- The emotional neglect from people who should have been protectors.
- The abandonment that left us questioning our worth.

Trauma occurs when something overwhelms your ability to cope and causes lasting emotional and spiritual damage.

You don't have to have visible scars to be broken inside.
You don't have to be dramatic to be deeply wounded.
You just have to be human—and honest enough to admit that life hit you hard.

TRIGGERS: THE ECHOES OF THE PAIN

A trigger is a present reminder of a past pain. It's the person, place, sound, scent, word, or experience that suddenly transports you back to the moment when the wound was first created.

Triggers aren't always loud. Sometimes, they come in whispers:

- Someone raising their voice reminds you of being yelled at as a child.
- Being excluded revives the feeling of rejection.
- Someone not texting back stirs the fear of abandonment.
- Constructive criticism feels like a personal attack.

Your body remembers—even when your mind forgets.

But the presence of a trigger is not a sign that you're weak. It's a sign that you're still healing. And healing means facing those triggers with grace, not shame.

GOD IS NOT AFRAID OF YOUR WOUNDS

Let's be clear: **Your trauma does not disqualify you. It draws God closer.** Psalm 147:3 says, *"He healeth the broken in heart, and bindeth up their wounds."*

Jesus never ran from the wounded—He ran toward them.

- He touched the leper.
- He sat with the Samaritan woman.
- He wept with Mary and Martha.
- He defended the adulterous woman from public shame.
- He restored Peter after denial.
- He healed the bleeding woman's body and her soul.

He doesn't just want to rescue you from survival—He wants to restore what you lost while you were in it.

THE LIE TRAUMA TELLS YOU

The enemy uses trauma to whisper lies:

- "You're not enough."
- "No one will ever love you."
- "You'll always be abandoned."
- "If they knew the real you, they'd leave."
- "You have to stay in control or you'll be hurt again."

And so, you build walls. Not boundaries—*walls*. The kind that keeps even God at a distance.

But here's the truth: God never asked you to carry what you've been carrying. He wants the pain, disappointment, shame, fear—*all of it*. Not to punish you. Not to expose you. But to *heal you*.

LET'S TRACE THE WOUND

Take a moment and reflect. When did you first start to shut down? When did trust start to feel unsafe? When did hope begin to feel foolish?

Was it after the heartbreak? After the divorce? After the miscarriage? After the church hurt? After the parent walked away? After the job loss? After the silence of God when you prayed the hardest?

Naming the source of your pain is the beginning of reclaiming your healing.

JOSEPH: BETRAYED BUT NOT BROKEN

Joseph in the Bible knew trauma all too well.

- Betrayed by his own brothers.
- Sold into slavery.
- Falsely accused.
- Forgotten in prison.

And yet, when he finally stood in power, his first response wasn't vengeance—it was **grace**. Why? Because he didn't stay stuck in the trauma, he allowed the process to purify his heart and posture him for promotion. He saw his pain through the lens of God's purpose.

Genesis 50:20: *"You intended to harm me, but God intended it for good to accomplish what is now being done, the saving of many lives." (NIV).*

God will use what was meant to destroy you as the very thing that develops you.

YOU'RE ALLOWED TO HEAL

You are allowed to:

- Grieve what hurt you.
- Feel what you've buried.
- Acknowledge what you've survived.
- Stop minimizing what broke your heart.
- Take up space in your own healing journey.

You are not weak for being wounded. You are strong for still showing up.

Healing is not denial. It is facing the truth, processing it in God's presence, and releasing the pain to make room for purpose.

TODAY'S FREEDOM TRUTH

You didn't choose what happened. But you can choose to stop living from that place.

The trauma is real—but so is your healing.

God is not looking for perfection. He's looking for your permission to go deeper. To deal with the root. To restore what survival mode tried to bury.

Your breakthrough begins with brutal honesty and bold hope.

SCRIPTURES FOR REFLECTION

But as for you, ye thought evil against me; but God meant it unto good, to bring to pass, as it is this day, to save much people alive. —Genesis 50:20

He healeth the broken in heart, and bindeth up their wounds. —Psalm 147:3

The Spirit of the Lord God is upon me; because the Lord hath anointed me to preach good tidings unto the meek; he hath sent me to bind up the brokenhearted, to proclaim liberty to the captives, and the opening of the prison to them that are bound; —Isaiah 61:1

And ye shall know the truth, and the truth shall make you free. —John 8:32

And be not conformed to this world: but be ye transformed by the renewing of your mind, that ye may prove what is that good, and acceptable, and perfect, will of God. —Romans 12:2

DECLARATION

I will not be defined by my trauma. I am not what happened to me. I am who God says I am—healed, whole, and called. I release shame, guilt, fear, and false responsibility. My healing matters. My story matters. And the truth of God's love will carry me into freedom.

CHAPTER 4

THE SPIRITUAL SIDE OF SURVIVAL

S urvival is more than a psychological or emotional state—it's deeply spiritual. What you fight in your mind and feel in your body often reflects a deeper war being waged in your spirit. Survival mode isn't just about past trauma—it's about how that trauma interrupted your connection with God, distorted your view of Him, and clouded your ability to hear His voice.

This is where the real war begins.

Survival mode can create a false theology: one where God seems silent, absent, or even punishing. But your pain was never proof of God's abandonment. It was proof of the brokenness of this world— a brokenness that Jesus came to redeem.

THE ENEMY ATTACKS IN SEASONS OF VULNERABILITY

When we're in survival mode, we are spiritually vulnerable. The enemy knows this, and he takes advantage of it:

- He plants lies that God has forgotten you.
- He convinces you that you're too damaged to be used.

- He whispers that faith doesn't work because your prayers weren't answered the way you hoped.
- He points to your pain as "evidence" that God doesn't care.

But this is where discernment matters.

Satan doesn't just want to harm your body—he wants to hijack your *beliefs*. If he can change the way you see God, he can keep you stuck in fear, bitterness, doubt, and shame.

Ephesians 6:12: *"For our struggle is not against flesh and blood, but against the rulers, against the authorities, against the powers of this dark world..." (NIV).*

This is not just emotional warfare. It's spiritual.

WHEN YOU STOP PRAYING LIKE YOU USED TO

Have you noticed that in survival mode, your prayers change?

- You stop asking boldly.
- You lower your expectations to avoid disappointment.
- You pray for endurance rather than breakthrough.
- You lose intimacy with God and settle for formality.
- You pray from fear instead of from faith.

But survival prayer is often silent. You go from seeking to simply *surviving*. You stop dreaming, and you start dreading. But even in this quiet place—God still listens. God still waits. God still whispers hope.

The enemy may want you to think God is distant. But survival mode doesn't cancel God's promises. It just blinds you from seeing them.

BIBLICAL PATTERNS: GOD IN THE WILDERNESS

The wilderness is the ultimate metaphor for spiritual survival. Over and over, we see it:

- **Moses** fled to the wilderness and met God in the burning bush.
- **David** hid in caves but wrote psalms that would change generations.
- **Jesus** fasted in the wilderness and defeated Satan's temptation.
- **Hagar**, desperate in the desert, encountered God as *El Roi*— the God who sees.

The wilderness is not a place of punishment—it's often a place of **preparation**. A sacred space where God strips away the noise, the dependencies, the idols, and the false securities—so you can learn to trust Him again.

Deuteronomy 8:2: *"Remember how the Lord your God led you through the wilderness for these forty years, humbling you and testing you to prove your character, and to find out whether or not you would obey his commands." (NLT).*

Your survival season is not a spiritual failure. It's an invitation to rediscover God in a deeper way.

SPIRITUAL NUMBNESS IS REAL

Let's address a truth many are afraid to admit: survival mode can make you spiritually numb.

You still go to church.
You still serve.
You still listen to sermons.
But your heart isn't engaged.
You don't expect God to speak.
You've been disappointed before, so now you stay guarded.

Spiritual numbness is a protective mechanism. You convince yourself it's better to not feel at all than to feel deeply and be let down. But God doesn't want numb followers—He wants hearts fully alive.

Ezekiel 36:26: *"I will give you a new heart and put a new spirit in you; I will remove from you your heart of stone..." (NIV).*

He wants to awaken your heart again. To revive your passion for His presence. To restore your ability to hope.

THE RESTORATION PROCESS STARTS IN THE SPIRIT

You cannot heal emotionally while remaining disconnected spiritually.

You cannot thrive mentally while ignoring your soul's deep hunger.

Healing your relationship with God is the *root* of healing everything else.

Here's what spiritual restoration might look like:

- Talking to God honestly—even if you're angry.
- Sitting in silence, letting Him speak.
- Worshiping through tears, even when you feel broken.
- Reading the Word, not for information, but for transformation.
- Asking for the Holy Spirit to reawaken what's gone cold in you.

You don't need to return to religion. You need to return to *relationship*.

JESUS IS STILL THE HEALER

Jesus doesn't just heal bodies. He heals **souls**.

Luke 4:18b: *"He has sent me to proclaim freedom for the prisoners and recovery of sight for the blind, to set the oppressed free..."* *(NIV)*.

Oppression doesn't always come in chains. Sometimes it comes in silence. In numbness. In survival. But Jesus breaks those chains too.

He is not disappointed in your survival season. He understands it— and He is calling you out of it with compassion, not condemnation.

A SPIRITUAL WAKE-UP CALL

You've been surviving in your own strength long enough. It's time to lean on God again—not as a distant deity, but as your Father, your Deliverer, Defender, and Healer.

Let the walls fall.
Let your heart soften.
Let His love go deeper than your fear.
Your spirit has been longing for air. Breathe again.

SCRIPTURES FOR REFLECTION

For we wrestle not against flesh and blood, but against principalities, against powers, against the rulers of the darkness of this world, against spiritual wickedness in high places. —Ephesians 6:12

And thou shalt remember all the way which the Lord thy God led thee these forty years in the wilderness, to humble thee, and to prove thee, to know what was in thine heart, whether thou wouldest keep his commandments, or no. —Deuteronomy 8:2

A new heart also will I give you, and a new spirit will I put within you: and I will take away the stony heart out of your flesh, and I will give you an heart of flesh. —Ezekiel 36:26

The Spirit of the Lord is upon me, because he hath anointed me to preach the gospel to the poor; he hath sent me to heal the brokenhearted, to preach deliverance to the captives, and recovering of sight to the blind, to set at liberty them that are bruised, —Luke 4:18

As the hart panteth after the water brooks, so panteth my soul after thee, O God. —Psalm 42:1

Likewise the Spirit also helpeth our infirmities: for we know not what we should pray for as we ought: but the Spirit itself maketh intercession for us with groanings which cannot be uttered. — Romans 8:26

DECLARATION

My spirit will no longer live in survival mode. I release numbness, fear, and religious performance. I receive fresh fire, fresh intimacy, and deep healing. I am spiritually awakening. God is near, and I am drawing close again. I trust Him not only with my survival—but with my future.

CHAPTER 5

RESETTING YOUR IDENTITY

When life throws blow after blow—when trauma, betrayal, loss, or disappointment knock the wind out of you—your identity often takes the hardest hit.

You start to confuse what happened **to you** with who you are.
You begin to live from wounds instead of from worth.
You wear labels that were never yours to begin with.

And slowly, survival mode convinces you that your identity is based on your pain, not your purpose.

This chapter is about divine realignment. It's time to hit the reset button on how you see yourself—because you can't live fully if you're still identifying yourself by a broken past.

WHO TOLD YOU THAT?

One of the most profound questions God asks in the Bible is found in Genesis 3:11. After Adam and Eve sinned and covered themselves in shame, God said: **"Who told thee that thou wast naked?"**

In other words: *Who told you something about yourself that I never said?*

That's the question you need to confront today.

Who told you that you were:

- Too damaged?
- Not enough?
- Unworthy of love?
- Just a survivor, not a success?
- A failure?
- Forgotten?

Every lie you've internalized about yourself is rooted in a moment of pain. But just because it felt true doesn't mean it *is* true.

SURVIVAL MODE TAINTS IDENTITY

When you're in survival mode, you often make decisions based on fear, not identity. You react instead of respond. You adapt instead of stand firm. You shrink instead of soar.

You wear masks to protect yourself.
You create personas to fit in.
You become who people need you to be—while forgetting who *God* created you to be.

But when the storm is over, and the masks are removed—*who are you?*

God is calling you back to your *original blueprint*—before heartbreak, before trauma, before rejection, before loss. He wants to reset your identity based on *His truth*, not your experience.

BIBLICAL EXAMPLES OF IDENTITY REWRITTEN

Throughout scripture, we see God redefine people who were stuck in survival:

- **Gideon** called himself the "least" of his family—God called him *a mighty warrior* (see Judges 6:15).
- **Moses** stuttered and doubted—God called him *a deliverer*.
- **Ruth** was a widowed outsider—God made her a key part of the Messiah's lineage.
- **Peter** denied Jesus—God called him *the rock* on which the church would be built.
- **Paul** persecuted Christians—God transformed him into *an apostle of grace*.

God doesn't consult your past when He determines your identity.

He speaks from your future.

THE IDENTITY CRISIS OF TRAUMA

One of the deepest wounds of trauma is that it makes you question who you are.

- Abuse makes you feel powerless.
- Rejection makes you feel unlovable.
- Abandonment makes you feel forgettable.
- Betrayal makes you feel foolish.

- Failure makes you feel like a fraud.

And if you're not careful, you'll wear those false identities for so long that they feel permanent.

But hear this: **what happened to you is a chapter—it's not your name.**

WHO DOES GOD SAY YOU ARE?

God has already spoken identity over you:

- You are *chosen* (see 1 Peter 2:9).
- You are *redeemed* (see Ephesians 1:7).
- You are *forgiven* (see Colossians 1:13–14).
- You are *more than a conqueror* (see Romans 8:37).
- You are *God's workmanship* (see Ephesians 2:10).
- You are *sealed with purpose* (see Ephesians 1:13).
- You are *loved with an everlasting love* (see Jeremiah 31:3).

You are not your survival story.
You are not your brokenness.
You are not your worst season.
You are who *God says* you are.

THE PROCESS OF IDENTITY RESTORATION

Resetting your identity doesn't happen overnight. It's a process—spiritual, emotional, mental. But it begins with choosing to:

1. **Reject the lies** you've believed about yourself.
2. **Replace them** with God's truth from His Word.

3. **Rebuild your mindset** around who you are in Christ.

Here's how you start:

- Write down the lies that have shaped your identity.
- Find scripture that directly contradicts those lies.
- Speak those scriptures aloud daily.
- Ask the Holy Spirit to help you see yourself the way He sees you.

This is not self-help. This is *soul alignment*.

IDENTITY FUELS DESTINY

Until you know who you are, you'll keep settling for less than you deserve.

- You'll stay in toxic relationships because you don't believe you deserve healthy ones.
- You'll sabotage opportunities because you don't believe you're capable.
- You'll keep your dreams small because you don't believe you're worthy of impact.

But your identity is the gateway to your destiny. When you believe who God says you are, everything shifts. You start praying differently, walking differently, living differently.

You stop begging for scraps—and start living like a child of the King.

TIME TO REINTRODUCE YOURSELF

The version of you that survived—thank them.
The version of you that endured—honor them.
But now, it's time to reintroduce the *real* you.
The healed you.
The whole you.
The confident, called, and fearless you.
Your identity is not a project to fix.
It's a treasure to rediscover.

SCRIPTURES FOR REFLECTION

And he said, Who told thee that thou wast naked? Hast thou eaten of the tree, whereof I commanded thee that thou shouldest not eat? —Genesis 3:11

And the angel of the Lord appeared unto him, and said unto him, The Lord is with thee, thou mighty man of valour. —Judges 6:12

But ye are a chosen generation, a royal priesthood, an holy nation, a peculiar people; that ye should shew forth the praises of him who hath called you out of darkness into his marvellous light; —1 Peter 2:9

Nay, in all these things we are more than conquerors through him that loved us. —Romans 8:37

For we are his workmanship, created in Christ Jesus unto good works, which God hath before ordained that we should walk in them. —Ephesians 2:10

For ye are dead, and your life is hid with Christ in God. —
Colossians 3:3

And the Gentiles shall see thy righteousness, and all kings thy glory:
and thou shalt be called by a new name, which the mouth of the
Lord shall name. —Isaiah 62:2

DECLARATION

I release every false identity formed in pain. I am not my past. I am
not my trauma. I am not my failure. I am who God says I am—
chosen, healed, loved, and whole. I reset my identity today by the
truth of God's Word. I live boldly, love freely, and walk in purpose
because I now know who I am.

CHAPTER 6

GOD'S PROMISE OF ABUNDANT LIFE

You ou weren't created just to make it. You were created to live. Fully. Freely. Abundantly.

The promise of God isn't limited to survival—it includes **abundance**. But for many of us, abundance feels unrealistic. Unreachable. Maybe even unholy. We've been conditioned to believe that if we have joy, peace, or overflow, we must be doing something wrong or being "too blessed" in a broken world.

But that mindset isn't humility—it's *bondage*.

You have permission to live in God's abundance—not just materially, but emotionally, spiritually, relationally, and mentally. The goal isn't perfection—it's fullness. A life that overflows with purpose, presence, and peace. Jesus Himself promised it.

THE ABUNDANT LIFE ISN'T A LUXURY—IT'S A PROMISE

John 10:10: *"The thief comes only to steal and kill and destroy; I have come that they may have life, and have it to the full." (NIV).*

This is the dividing line between survival and abundant living.

Survival mode is what the enemy uses to keep you stuck in fear, pain, and lack. Abundant life is what Jesus died to give you.

This life doesn't mean the absence of struggle—but it does mean the presence of overflowing purpose in the midst of it. It means:

- Peace that surpasses understanding.
- Joy that doesn't depend on circumstances.
- Identity that's rooted in grace, not performance.
- A future that is bright, no matter your past.

Jesus didn't come to help you manage trauma. He came to help you overcome it.

WHAT DOES ABUNDANT LIFE ACTUALLY LOOK LIKE?

Abundant life isn't just more stuff. It's more **substance**.

- A healed mind.
- A joyful heart.
- Relationships that honor and uplift.
- Spiritual clarity and strength.
- Living on assignment—not just by accident.
- Feeling safe enough to dream again.

Abundant life means walking in sync with heaven's rhythm. It's not without storms, but it comes with divine shelter. Not without battles, but with guaranteed victory. Not without losses, but with undeniable recovery.

BARRIERS THAT BLOCK ABUNDANT LIFE

So why don't more people experience this?

Because abundance isn't just received—it must be *believed*.

And too often, we allow internal barriers to block God's external blessings:

- **Guilt**: "I don't deserve abundance after what I've done."
- **Shame**: "People like me don't get to thrive."
- **Fear**: "If I let go of survival mode, I'll lose control."
- **Poverty mindsets**: "I just need enough to get by."
- **Religious trauma**: "God is only pleased when I suffer."

These lies keep us chained to lack. But the cross wasn't just about *saving* you—it was about *freeing* you to live in all God intended.

BIBLICAL EXAMPLES OF ABUNDANT LIFE

God has always been in the business of turning scarcity into overflow:

- He gave **Abraham** descendants as numerous as the stars.
- He led **Israel** to a land flowing with milk and honey.
- He provided **Elijah** with a never-ending jar of oil.
- He gave **Solomon** wisdom *and* wealth.
- He restored **Job's** life *double* after devastation.
- He turned **Peter's** night of empty nets into a morning of miraculous catch.
- He fed the **five thousand** with a few loaves—and had leftovers.

God's nature is abundant. His grace, His mercy, His goodness—
never run out.

LIVING FROM A PLACE OF OVERFLOW

God wants you to live from *overflow*, not from *exhaustion.*

Psalm 23:5b says, *"You anoint my head with oil; my cup
overflows." (NIV).*

Overflow isn't about excess—it's about **sufficiency with surplus**.
It means:

- You're not drained by people because you've been filled by
  God.
- You don't beg for affirmation because you know you're
  already accepted.
- You give love, joy, peace, and wisdom from a heart that has
  more than enough.

Survival mode says, "Just enough to get through the day."

Abundant living says, "I have more than enough to pour into
others."

MAKING ROOM FOR ABUNDANCE

To step into God's abundance, you have to *make room*:

- Clear the clutter of toxic thinking.
- Detox from survival language ("I'll never...", "I can't...").
- Release scarcity patterns from past generations.

- Open your heart to the possibility that life can be *beautiful again.*

God wants to trust you with more—but He needs your heart to be healed enough to handle it.

You don't have to beg for abundance. You just have to believe that it was always yours.

IT'S TIME TO RECEIVE

You've done enough surviving.
Now it's time to receive.
Not in fear. Not in guilt. Not in shame.
But in faith.
You were not created to struggle forever.
You were not designed to live beneath your calling.
You were made to reflect the goodness of God *through your life.*

This next season is not about fighting to stay alive. It's about *living* like you've already won—because in Christ, **you have**.

SCRIPTURES FOR REFLECTION

The thief cometh not, but for to steal, and to kill, and to destroy: I am come that they might have life, and that they might have it more abundantly. —John 10:10

Thou preparest a table before me in the presence of mine enemies: thou anointest my head with oil; my cup runneth over. —Psalm 23:5

And God is able to make all grace abound toward you; that ye, always having all sufficiency in all things, may abound to every good work: —2 Corinthians 9:8

Now unto him that is able to do exceeding abundantly above all that we ask or think, according to the power that worketh in us, — Ephesians 3:20

Wherefore do ye spend money for that which is not bread? and your labour for that which satisfieth not? hearken diligently unto me, and eat ye that which is good, and let your soul delight itself in fatness. —Isaiah 55:2

So shall thy barns be filled with plenty, and thy presses shall burst out with new wine. —Proverbs 3:10

DECLARATION

I release survival and receive abundance. I believe that Jesus came to give me life—and life to the full. I am not bound by fear, lack, guilt, or shame. I walk in overflow, I expect increase, and I live with joy. I am no longer just surviving—I am living in the abundance God has already prepared for me.

CHAPTER 7

HEALING THE MIND AND SOUL

S urvival may begin in the body, but it settles in the mind and soul.

Long after the crisis ends, your thoughts can still carry its weight. Your emotions can still bleed from wounds no one else sees. And without intentional healing, you will continue living from a place of brokenness, even in a season meant for breakthrough.

You cannot step fully into life until your inner world is healed. The mind and the soul—your thoughts, feelings, memories, and spirit— must be renewed, refreshed, and restored by the power of God.

This chapter is about diving deep, not just into what happened, but into how it *shaped you*—and how it no longer has to define you.

THE MIND: WHERE SURVIVAL PATTERNS BEGIN

The mind is powerful. It is where beliefs are built. It is where fear is formed. It is where your worldview, identity, and emotional responses are shaped.

Romans 12:2 reminds us: **"be ye transformed by the renewing of your mind."**

Because your thoughts set the tone for your entire life.

In survival mode, your mind learns to:

- Anticipate danger.
- Expect the worst.
- Filter out joy.
- Replay past failures.
- Create internal "rules" to avoid getting hurt again.

Eventually, you're not living—you're scanning for threats. Even when no threats are present.

This is how people end up "blessed but broken." Surrounded by opportunity but bound in thought. Holding a Bible but believing they're beyond restoration.

But the healing of your mind begins with **new information** and **repeated affirmation**. You must unlearn the lies and relearn the truth.

THE SOUL: WHERE PAIN LINGERS

Your soul carries what your words never said.
Your soul remembers the childhood moment you were left out.
The conversation that crushed your confidence.
The night you cried yourself to sleep, asking God why.
The divorce.
The rejection.

The abuse.
The church hurt.

The time they said "I love you," and then proved they didn't.

These aren't just memories. These are soul wounds. And if left unhealed, they turn into:

- Bitterness
- Depression
- Anxiety
- Distrust
- Isolation
- Anger at God

But your soul isn't beyond healing. It's actually *craving* it.

SIGNS YOU NEED SOUL HEALING

- You're always exhausted, even with rest.
- You feel spiritually disconnected no matter how often you pray.
- You feel heavy but don't know why.
- You avoid intimacy and vulnerability.
- You constantly rehearse painful memories or "what ifs."
- You numb yourself emotionally (with food, distractions, isolation, etc.).
- You feel like joy is something for other people, not you.

These signs aren't weaknesses. They're *invitations*. Invitations to go deeper with God.

GOD CARES ABOUT YOUR MENTAL AND EMOTIONAL HEALTH

Don't believe the lie that mental and emotional healing is "less spiritual."

- Jesus wept.
- David wrote poetry from the depths of depression.
- Elijah asked to die under a tree.
- Paul wrestled with despair but clung to grace.

God created your mind. He created your soul. He knows when it's bruised, and He is not intimidated by your trauma. He is the only One who can heal it completely.

Psalm 23:3: *"He restoreth my soul:"*

God doesn't want to just *patch* your mind and soul. He wants to **restore** them—to their original purpose and power.

HEALING IS A PROCESS, NOT A SWITCH

You won't wake up one morning with all the pain gone. But you will wake up one morning and realize the pain doesn't own you anymore.

Healing takes time, but it also takes **intention**:

- **Prayer**: Honest, raw communication with God.
- **Scripture**: Replacing lies with truth.
- **Community**: Allowing trusted people to walk with you.
- **Therapy**: Receiving help without shame.

- **Forgiveness**: Releasing yourself and others.
- **Worship**: Releasing burdens and embracing God's presence.

You have to *engage* in your healing. You have to want wholeness more than you want revenge, justification, or safety behind your walls.

BREAKING CYCLES IN THE MIND

2 Corinthians 10:5 tells us to *"take captive every thought and make it obedient to Christ."*

You can't control what thoughts appear, but you can control how long they stay. Healing your mind requires:

- Challenging self-sabotaging thoughts.
- Choosing faith over fear-based conclusions.
- Catching internal lies and replacing them with God's Word.
- Speaking truth over your life out loud—until your heart catches up.

GOD IS STILL THE HEALER OF THE BROKEN

No matter how long you've been in emotional or mental pain, it's not too late.

Jeremiah 30:17: *"But I will restore you to health and heal your wounds, declares the Lord,"* *(NIV)*.

He's not afraid of what you've become in survival mode.
He still sees the *you* that existed before the pain.

He wants to restore you, not just for yourself, but so your life can be a testimony of what healing really looks like.

YOU'RE NOT BROKEN. YOU'RE BECOMING.

You may feel broken. But God sees someone *becoming*:

- Stronger in faith.
- Clearer in purpose.
- Softer in spirit.
- Wiser in decisions.
- Bolder in love.
- Freer in mind.
- Lighter in soul.

This is not the end. This is the beginning of your real life. The healed life. The whole life. The abundant life.

Healing isn't easy. But it's always worth it.

SCRIPTURES FOR REFLECTION

And be not conformed to this world: but be ye transformed by the renewing of your mind, that ye may prove what is that good, and acceptable, and perfect, will of God. —Romans 12:2

He restoreth my soul: he leadeth me in the paths of righteousness for his name's sake. —Psalm 23:3

For I will restore health unto thee, and I will heal thee of thy wounds, saith the Lord; because they called thee an Outcast, saying, This is Zion, whom no man seeketh after. —Jeremiah 30:17

Casting down imaginations, and every high thing that exalteth itself against the knowledge of God, and bringing into captivity every thought to the obedience of Christ; —2 Corinthians 10:5

The Spirit of the Lord God is upon me; because the Lord hath anointed me to preach good tidings unto the meek; he hath sent me to bind up the brokenhearted, to proclaim liberty to the captives, and the opening of the prison to them that are bound; —Isaiah 61:1

And the peace of God, which passeth all understanding, shall keep your hearts and minds through Christ Jesus. —Philippians 4:7

DECLARATION

I speak healing over my mind and soul. I am no longer bound by fear, anxiety, shame, or depression. I take every thought captive and align it with the truth of God's Word. I am being restored from the inside out. My thoughts are renewed. My heart is light. My soul is healing, and my future is bright. I am whole—by the power and love of Jesus Christ.

CHAPTER 8

STEPPING OUT OF THE WILDERNESS

There comes a moment in every survivor's life when the wilderness becomes too familiar.

It's not that you're still in crisis. It's that you've adjusted to living *as if* you are. You've gotten used to wandering—used to waiting, used to the quiet, used to being stuck. But the wilderness was never supposed to be a permanent address. It was a process, not a destination.

God allowed the wilderness to grow you—not to bury you.

Now it's time to step out.

WHAT IS THE WILDERNESS SEASON?

Biblically, the wilderness is a place of testing, transformation, and transition.

- It's where **Moses** heard God speak.
- It's where **Israel** was refined and prepared.
- It's where **Jesus** fasted and resisted temptation.

- It's where people wrestled with purpose, identity, and obedience.

In the wilderness:

- Resources are limited.
- Direction can feel unclear.
- Progress is slow.
- And survival mode feels like the only way to cope.

But even in its discomfort, the wilderness has purpose. It reveals what's inside of you, exposes what can't go with you, and prepares you for the next level of promise.

GOD WAS WITH YOU IN THE WILDERNESS

Even when the Israelites were in the wilderness for 40 years, God didn't abandon them. In fact, He:

- Gave them food from heaven (manna).
- Provided water from rocks.
- Led them with a pillar of cloud by day and fire by night.
- Ensured their clothes and shoes never wore out.

Deuteronomy 29:5: *"During the forty years that I led you through the wilderness, your clothes did not wear out, nor did the sandals on your feet." (NIV).*

This reminds us that even when life feels stagnant or dry, God still sustains. And when the season changes, He doesn't just sustain— He launches.

WHY SOME PEOPLE STAY TOO LONG

Many people get used to the wilderness. It becomes safe. Predictable. Controlled. After all, in the wilderness:

- You don't have to risk disappointment.
- You don't have to step into unfamiliar territory.
- You don't have to fight giants.
- You don't have to expand your faith.

But comfort in the wilderness is dangerous. It convinces you that *this* is all there is.

When God told the Israelites, *"You have stayed long enough at this mountain"* (see Deuteronomy 1:6), it was a call to move—not just physically, but *mentally and spiritually.*

Sometimes we're not waiting on God. He's waiting for *us* to take the first step.

THE SIGNS IT'S TIME TO MOVE FORWARD

You may be sensing the shift if:

- Old strategies no longer work.
- You feel spiritually restless.
- God is stirring new desires in your heart.
- You're frustrated without understanding why.
- You sense that "there has to be more than this."

These aren't signs of failure—they're *signs of transition*. The cloud is moving. The fire is shifting. The grace for the old season is lifting, and a new assignment is calling.

LEAVING THE WILDERNESS MEANS FACING THE UNKNOWN

Let's be honest—stepping out is *scary*. The wilderness may have been dry, but it was familiar. It's hard to walk away from something—even dysfunction—when it's predictable.

But stepping into promise always requires:

- Courage
- Obedience
- Trust
- And willingness to let go of what no longer serves you.

Joshua 1:9: *"This is my command—be strong and courageous! Do not be afraid or discouraged. For the Lord your God is with you wherever you go." (NLT).*

You're not walking out alone. God goes before you.

THE PROMISED LAND REQUIRES A NEW MINDSET

The Israelites couldn't enter the promised land until the wilderness mentality was broken. A new land demands a new level of faith, responsibility, and vision.

You cannot possess Canaan with an Egypt mindset.

- You can't walk into overflow still expecting lack.
- You can't step into healthy relationships while clinging to abandonment fears.
- You can't embrace calling while still doubting your identity.

That's why healing matters. That's why renewing your mind matters. The wilderness may have taught you how to survive, but now it's time to learn how to *live*.

PRACTICAL STEPS TO STEP OUT

1. Acknowledge the Shift

Name the season you're in. Declare that the wilderness has served its purpose.

2. Obey the Next Instruction

God may not give you the full picture, but He always gives the next step. Take it.

3. Let Go of What Can't Go With You

Some people, habits, and mentalities cannot cross over with you.

4. Feed Yourself Differently

In the wilderness, God provided manna. In the promised land, they had to plant, grow, and harvest. Be ready to *work* for the promise.

5. Walk with Boldness

Don't creep out of the wilderness—*walk out with authority*. You survived. Now thrive.

YOU'RE NOT WHO YOU WERE WHEN YOU WENT IN

You went into the wilderness broken—but you're coming out *built.*
You went in doubting—but you're coming out *determined.*
You went in hurt—but you're coming out *healed.*
You went in barely breathing—but you're coming out *bold.*
The wilderness refined you. But it does not define you.
You're stepping into purpose. Into peace. Into provision.

Step forward. The land is waiting.

SCRIPTURES FOR REFLECTION

The Lord our God spake unto us in Horeb, saying, Ye have dwelt long enough in this mount: —Deuteronomy 1:6

And I have led you forty years in the wilderness: your clothes are not waxen old upon you, and thy shoe is not waxen old upon thy foot. —Deuteronomy 29:5

Have not I commanded thee? Be strong and of a good courage; be not afraid, neither be thou dismayed: for the Lord thy God is with thee whithersoever thou goest. —Joshua 1:9

Behold, I will do a new thing; now it shall spring forth; shall ye not know it? I will even make a way in the wilderness, and rivers in the desert. —Isaiah 43:19

And he led them forth by the right way, that they might go to a city of habitation. —Psalm 107:7

By faith Abraham, when he was called to go out into a place which he should after receive for an inheritance, obeyed; and he went out, not knowing whither he went. —Hebrews 11:8

DECLARATION

I am stepping out of the wilderness. I release fear, delay, and comfort zones. I declare this is my season to move forward with courage. I walk by faith, not by sight. God is leading me into promise, purpose, and peace. I am no longer wandering—I am walking boldly into my destiny.

CHAPTER 9

EMBRACING JOY WITHOUT FEAR

For those who have lived in survival mode, **joy** often feels like a luxury—or worse, a trap.

When you've spent years in pain, disappointment, or trauma, joy doesn't come naturally. It feels foreign, fleeting, maybe even dangerous. You expect the worst to follow the good, so you don't allow yourself to fully feel it. You wait for the shoe to drop. You brace for heartbreak before happiness can settle in.

But, friend, God never intended for your joy to be temporary, tainted, or timid. He created you with joy in mind. **Joy is not just a feeling—it's a divine strength.**

JOY IS NOT FRAGILE—IT'S A WEAPON

Nehemiah 8:10: *"Do not grieve, for the joy of the Lord is your strength." (NIV).*

Joy is not soft. It's not shallow. It's not naïve.
Joy is powerful. It's fierce. It's resilient.

Survival mode may have taught you to live cautiously, but joy teaches you to live courageously. To laugh again. To dance again. To hope again. Not because life is perfect—but because God is present.

Your joy is not found in circumstances—it's found in Christ.

FEAR HAS STOLEN YOUR LAUGHTER LONG ENOUGH

Let's be honest: when you've been through deep pain, joy feels risky.

- "What if it doesn't last?"
- "What if I let my guard down and get hurt again?"
- "What if it's taken away like everything else?"

So you settle for moments of relief instead of lifestyles of joy. But that's not the life Jesus offers.

John 15:11: *"I have told you this so that my joy may be in you and that your joy may be complete." (NIV).*

Complete joy. Not fractured. Not temporary. *Complete.*

You don't have to choose between being wise and being joyful. You can have both. Joy doesn't deny pain—it refuses to be *defined* by it.

JOY THAT SURVIVES THE FIRE

Let's remember people in scripture who experienced deep suffering—but still found joy:

- **David**, who wrote songs of praise while hiding in caves.
- **Paul and Silas**, who sang hymns while chained in a prison.
- **Jesus**, who endured the cross *"for the joy set before Him"* (see Hebrews 12:2).

Joy is not about what's happening *around* you—it's about what's happening *within* you. It is spiritual resistance. It is heaven's rebellion against hell's plan for your life.

When you choose joy, you are saying: *"I believe God is still good, even when life is hard."*

WHY YOU MAY BE SABOTAGING YOUR OWN JOY

Sometimes we unknowingly block joy because of:

- **Guilt**: "How can I be happy after what happened?"
- **Grief**: "If I laugh, it dishonors my pain or my loved ones."
- **Control**: "If I feel joy, I'm not prepared for disappointment."
- **Unworthiness**: "I don't deserve joy."

These are all lies.
Joy does not erase your grief. It walks with it.
Joy does not mean you've forgotten the pain. It means you've decided not to be owned by it.

GIVE YOURSELF PERMISSION TO SMILE AGAIN

Some of you haven't laughed from your soul in years. You've smiled politely. You've chuckled to be polite. But deep, belly-aching, soul-freeing joy? It feels like a distant memory.

Today, give yourself permission to:

- Laugh without apologizing.
- Dance without explanation.
- Smile without suspicion.
- Celebrate without waiting for something to go wrong.

Joy doesn't mean everything is fixed. It means you're free even while things are still being healed.

CULTIVATING JOY EVERY DAY

Joy may begin as a supernatural gift, but it can be cultivated through intentional daily practice:

- **Gratitude**: Listing what you're thankful for—even in the storm.
- **Worship**: Not because you feel good, but because God *is* good.
- **Time in the Word**: Letting the promises of God rewire your perspective.
- **Sabbath rest**: Enjoying life, not just surviving it.
- **Laughter**: Watch something funny. Be around people who lift your spirit.
- **Presence**: Slow down. Savor moments. Be fully *here.*

Psalm 16:11: *"You make known to me the path of life; you will fill me with joy in your presence…" (NIV).*

JOY IS YOUR PORTION

You may have inherited pain, but you are not obligated to pass it on.

You may have experienced sorrow, but joy is your inheritance in Christ.

Isaiah 61:3 says He gives us *"the oil of joy instead of mourning."*
That's an *exchange*—not a suggestion.

God is not asking you to pretend you're happy. He's inviting you to *embrace the joy that already belongs to you.*
Even if you're still healing.
Even if you're still rebuilding.
Even if you're still afraid.
Joy and healing can walk hand in hand.

YOU DESERVE TO FEEL GOOD AGAIN

Let that settle in: You deserve to feel good again.

Not because life is perfect—but because God is restoring you. And part of that restoration includes the return of your joy.

You're not just allowed to feel joy—you're *called* to carry it.

So lift your head.
Unclench your heart.
Take the walls down.
And let joy run wild again.

SCRIPTURES FOR REFLECTION

Then he said unto them, Go your way, eat the fat, and drink the sweet, and send portions unto them for whom nothing is prepared: for this day is holy unto our Lord: neither be ye sorry; for the joy of the Lord is your strength. —Nehemiah 8:10

These things have I spoken unto you, that my joy might remain in you, and that your joy might be full. —John 15:11

Thou wilt shew me the path of life: in thy presence is fulness of joy; at thy right hand there are pleasures for evermore. —Psalm 16:11

To appoint unto them that mourn in Zion, to give unto them beauty for ashes, the oil of joy for mourning, the garment of praise for the spirit of heaviness; that they might be called trees of righteousness, the planting of the Lord, that he might be glorified. —Isaiah 61:3

Looking unto Jesus the author and finisher of our faith; who for the joy that was set before him endured the cross, despising the shame, and is set down at the right hand of the throne of God. —Hebrews 12:2

Now the God of hope fill you with all joy and peace in believing, that ye may abound in hope, through the power of the Holy Ghost. —Romans 15:13

For his anger endureth but a moment; in his favour is life: weeping may endure for a night, but joy cometh in the morning. —Psalm 30:5

DECLARATION

I embrace joy without fear. I will not sabotage my happiness or shrink my hope. I receive the joy of the Lord as my strength. I laugh, I dance, I celebrate, and I live. My past does not cancel my joy. My pain does not disqualify my peace. Today, I walk in joy—freely, boldly, and without apology.

CHAPTER 11

BOUNDARIES THAT BUILD LIFE

When you've spent years in survival mode, boundaries can feel unfamiliar—or even wrong.

You may have been conditioned to equate love with overextension. To believe that saying "no" is selfish. To think that constant availability equals spiritual maturity. But here's the truth:

Boundaries don't push people away—boundaries protect what matters.

They are not walls to keep love out. They are gates to allow in only what nourishes your soul.

And if you're going to truly live—not just survive—you must learn to set boundaries that build, not break.

THE MISUNDERSTANDING OF BOUNDARIES

In religious circles, boundaries are often misunderstood. People equate self-denial with self-erasure. We're taught to "turn the other cheek," "bear each other's burdens," and "die to ourselves." All biblical principles—*in the right context.*

But none of those scriptures suggest abandoning **discernment, stewardship, or self-worth**.

Jesus Himself had boundaries:

- He withdrew to rest and pray (see Luke 5:16).
- He didn't heal everyone who asked (see John 5:1–15).
- He confronted toxic behavior (see Matthew 23).
- He walked away from crowds (see John 6:15).
- He allowed people to leave without chasing them (see John 6:66–67).

Jesus loved deeply—and yet, He didn't let everyone close.

WHY SURVIVORS STRUGGLE WITH BOUNDARIES

If you've been in survival mode:

- You may fear that setting boundaries will lead to rejection.
- You may believe that your value comes from being needed.
- You may equate busyness with purpose.
- You may have grown up with blurred or nonexistent boundaries.

As a result, you may:

- Overgive until you're emotionally bankrupt.
- Allow people to violate your space, peace, or priorities.
- Say yes out of guilt instead of love.

- Confuse rescue with relationship.

But God isn't calling you to burn out in the name of serving others. He's calling you to serve from *wholeness, not depletion.*

WHAT BOUNDARIES ACTUALLY DO

1. Boundaries protect your peace.

You can't carry peace into chaos you weren't meant to fix.

2. Boundaries clarify expectations.

They let others know what's acceptable and what isn't.

3. Boundaries preserve your purpose.

Not every invitation aligns with your assignment.

4. Boundaries build healthy relationships.

Real love respects space, time, and limits.

5. Boundaries protect your healing.

You can't heal in environments that keep reopening the wound.

BIBLICAL BOUNDARY PRINCIPLES

1. Proverbs 4:23 – *"Keep thy heart with all diligence; for out of it are the issues of life."*

Pastor Dr. Claudine Benjamin

Guarding your heart isn't being cold—it's being wise.

2. **Ecclesiastes 3:1** – *"To every thing there is a season, and a time to every purpose under the heaven:"*

Saying "not now" isn't rejection—it's rhythm.

3. **Galatians 6:5** – *"For every man shall bear his own burden."*

You are not responsible for carrying what others refuse to.

4. **Matthew 5:37** – *"But let your communication be, Yea, yea; Nay, nay: for whatsoever is more than these cometh of evil."*

Clear, honest boundaries are holy.

HOW TO BEGIN SETTING LIFE-BUILDING BOUNDARIES

1. Assess What Drains You

Who or what makes you feel resentful, anxious, or manipulated? That's a sign of a boundary breach.

2. Start Small and Be Clear

Boundaries don't need long explanations. A simple, "I'm not able to do that right now," is powerful.

3. Don't Over-Explain or Apologize

Your "no" is enough. Guilt is not required.

4. Prepare for Pushback

When you start protecting yourself, those who benefitted from your lack of boundaries may resist. That's okay. *Hold your ground with grace.*

5. Set Boundaries with Yourself Too

This includes rest, diet, spiritual discipline, digital habits, and thought patterns. Boundaries are also internal.

BOUNDARIES ARE NOT ABOUT CONTROL—THEY'RE ABOUT STEWARDSHIP

When God created the earth, He established boundaries:

- Light and dark
- Land and sea
- Time and seasons
- Work and rest

Boundaries were the **first act of order** in creation.

When you begin to establish boundaries in your own life, you are mirroring God's original design: **to bring order, peace, and protection to what is precious.**

And your peace is precious.
Your calling is precious.
Your healing is precious.
Your heart is precious.

LETTING GO OF GUILT AND EMBRACING FREEDOM

You are not selfish for setting boundaries.
You are not unloving for choosing rest.
You are not wrong for saying "enough."

Boundaries do not disconnect you from love—they help you love *well.*
Boundaries do not hinder your calling—they help you stay *focused.*
You do not need permission to protect your peace.
You already have it—from heaven.

SCRIPTURES FOR REFLECTION

And he withdrew himself into the wilderness, and prayed. —Luke 5:16

Keep thy heart with all diligence; for out of it are the issues of life. —Proverbs 4:23

To every thing there is a season, and a time to every purpose under the heaven: —Ecclesiastes 3:1

For every man shall bear his own burden. —Galatians 6:5

But let your communication be, Yea, yea; Nay, nay: for whatsoever is more than these cometh of evil. —Matthew 5:37

And my people shall dwell in a peaceable habitation, and in sure dwellings, and in quiet resting places; —Isaiah 32:18

DECLARATION

I am no longer afraid to set boundaries. I release guilt, fear, and the need to please everyone. I guard my heart with wisdom and strength. I choose peace, clarity, and rest. I honor what God is doing in my life by protecting my space, spirit, and soul. My boundaries build a life of freedom, focus, and fulfillment.

CHAPTER 12

WHOLENESS IS YOUR BIRTHRIGHT

You were not born broken.

You were born in God's image—created for connection, crafted with purpose, and called to walk in wholeness. Life may have wounded you. Experiences may have distorted you. People may have mishandled you. But your **original design**—the one authored by God Himself—was never broken. It was whole.

And the good news? What life fractured, **God restores**.

Wholeness is not a fantasy reserved for the perfect. Wholeness is your *birthright* in Christ. It is not about having a life free from pain—it's about living with a healed heart and a sound mind in the *midst* of it.

YOU WERE MADE TO BE WHOLE, NOT JUST FUNCTIONING

Too often, we confuse functioning with healing. We assume that because we're getting things done—working, parenting, attending church, running businesses—we must be fine.

But functioning isn't freedom.

Performing isn't peace.
And being busy isn't the same as being *whole*.

Wholeness is the divine alignment of your mind, body, soul, and spirit.

It's the restoration of your heart, the renewal of your mind, and the reconnecting of your purpose to your identity.

JESUS CAME TO MAKE YOU WHOLE

When Jesus healed, He didn't just stop at the physical. He went deeper.

In Luke 17, Jesus healed ten lepers. But only *one* came back to thank Him. And to that one, Jesus didn't just say, "You're healed." He said, *"Your faith has made you **whole**"* (see Luke 17:19).

There's a difference.

- Healing stops the bleeding.
- **Wholeness restores what was lost.**
- Healing soothes the wound.
- **Wholeness brings back your strength.**
- Healing ends the pain.
- **Wholeness gives you your life back.**

Jesus didn't just want them physically well—He wanted them **emotionally, spiritually, and relationally restored.**

YOU CAN'T INHERIT WHOLENESS WHILE HOLDING ON TO BROKENNESS

Wholeness requires surrender.

You cannot walk in wholeness and still cling to:

- Old trauma identities
- Toxic connections
- Destructive thought patterns
- Bitterness and unforgiveness
- Shame and guilt

You can't hold hands with your past and still move forward in your future.

Isaiah 43:18–19a: *"Forget the former things; do not dwell on the past. See, I am doing a new thing!" (NIV).*

Wholeness requires trust—trust that what God has for you is greater than what you've been through.

SIGNS YOU'RE WALKING TOWARD WHOLENESS

Wholeness doesn't mean you never hurt again. It means your pain no longer *owns* you.

Here's what it looks like:

- You can talk about what happened without breaking down.
- You forgive without needing an apology.
- You set boundaries without guilt.

87

- You rest without shame.
- You experience joy without fear.
- You love again without constantly expecting abandonment.

Wholeness is not perfection.

Wholeness is peace with your past, presence in your now, and hope for your future.

WHOLENESS ISN'T EARNED—IT'S RECEIVED

You don't have to work harder to be whole.
You don't have to perform better.
You don't have to fake healing for the sake of appearances.
You simply have to *believe that it's possible* and invite God into the broken places.

Jeremiah 30:17: *"But I will restore you to health and heal your wounds, declares the Lord..." (NIV).*

He wants to put the shattered pieces of your life back together—and make it more beautiful than it was before the breaking.

WHOLENESS IMPACTS EVERY AREA OF LIFE

When you begin to walk in wholeness, everything changes:

- Your relationships become healthier because you're not projecting pain.
- Your decisions become clearer because they're not driven by fear.

- Your habits shift because you no longer need to numb or distract yourself.
- Your vision expands because you're no longer stuck in survival.

Wholeness gives you the capacity to carry the weight of destiny without it crushing you.

You stop leaking from old wounds.
You stop settling because you're scared.
You stop hiding behind performance.

And you begin to live—truly live—as God always intended.

DECLARE WAR ON THE BELIEF THAT YOU'RE TOO BROKEN

The enemy wants you to believe that wholeness is unreachable for *people like you.*

Too far gone.
Too scarred.
Too used.
Too much.

But those are lies rooted in shame—and shame is *not* your portion.
Grace is.

Restoration is.
Wholeness is.

If God can restore the years the locusts have eaten (see Joel 2:25), then surely He can restore *you.*

YOUR WHOLENESS WILL SET OTHERS FREE

Don't forget—your healing is not just for you.
Your wholeness becomes a testimony for others still stuck in their survival.
You become the evidence that healing is possible.
You become the voice that says, "Me too… and God brought me through."
You become a safe place for others to believe again.
You don't just live healed—you live as a healer.

SCRIPTURES FOR REFLECTION

And he said unto him, Arise, go thy way: thy faith hath made thee whole. —Luke 17:19

For I will restore health unto thee, and I will heal thee of thy wounds, saith the Lord; because they called thee an Outcast, saying, This is Zion, whom no man seeketh after. —Jeremiah 30:17

Remember ye not the former things, neither consider the things of old. Behold, I will do a new thing; now it shall spring forth; shall ye not know it? I will even make a way in the wilderness, and rivers in the desert. —Isaiah 43:18–19

He healeth the broken in heart, and bindeth up their wounds. — Psalm 147:3

And I will restore to you the years that the locust hath eaten, the cankerworm, and the caterpiller, and the palmerworm, my great army which I sent among you. —Joel 2:25

Being confident of this very thing, that he which hath begun a good work in you will perform it until the day of Jesus Christ: — Philippians 1:6

DECLARATION

Wholeness is my birthright. I am not defined by brokenness. I release guilt, shame, and every false identity. I receive God's restoration in every area of my life—mind, soul, body, and spirit. I will not merely survive—I will thrive in wholeness. I am healed, I am whole, and I am walking in the fullness of who God created me to be.

CHAPTER 13

RELATIONSHIPS BEYOND SURVIVAL

Survival mode impacts not only how we view ourselves, but how we relate to others.

When you've lived on edge, when you've been hurt, abandoned, betrayed, or misused—your relationships become shaped by *defense*, not *connection*. You learn how to protect, but not how to receive. You become skilled at avoiding pain but struggle to welcome love. You maintain surface-level closeness while your heart remains guarded beneath layers of self-preservation.

But as you step into your healed life, your relationships must also shift—from survival to sincerity, from fear to freedom, from defense to divine connection.

You are called to **relationships that reflect healing, not just history**.

SURVIVAL MODE TEACHES YOU TO DISCONNECT

In survival mode, relationships often serve as:

- **Coping mechanisms** rather than connections.
- **Distractions** rather than destiny partners.
- **Emotional dumping grounds** rather than mutual support systems.
- **Validation vending machines** rather than spaces of real intimacy.

You might:

- Struggle to trust, even when people haven't hurt you.
- Keep people at a distance, even though you crave closeness.
- Over-give to earn love or stay relevant.
- Tolerate toxic dynamics out of fear of abandonment.
- Sabotage good relationships because you feel unworthy.

But survival mode doesn't get to decide how you do relationships anymore.

GOD CREATED YOU FOR CONNECTION, NOT CODEPENDENCY

You were never meant to walk alone.

Even in Eden—before sin, pain, or trauma—God said, *"It is not good for man to be alone"* (see Genesis 2:18).

Your need for connection is not a weakness—it's a divine design.

But connection is not the same as codependency.

Codependency says: "I need you to complete me, define me, or keep me together."

Healthy connection says: "I am whole in God, and I choose to walk with you in love and truth."

Relationships built in survival mode focus on rescue.
Relationships built in healing focus on *reciprocity*.

WHAT HEALED RELATIONSHIPS LOOK LIKE

When you're living beyond survival, relationships begin to look different:

- There is **honest communication**, not passive-aggressive silence.
- There is **mutual respect**, not silent suffering.
- There is **accountability**, not enabling.
- There is **space for growth**, not pressure to perform.
- There is **joy in presence**, not anxiety from perfectionism.
- There is **freedom**, not fear.

1 Corinthians 13:7: *"Love never gives up, never loses faith, is always hopeful, and endures through every circumstance." (NLT).*

Real love doesn't control. It doesn't manipulate. It makes room— for grace, truth, and growth.

FRIENDSHIP AFTER THE STORM

Many survivors of trauma or prolonged struggle find it hard to build or rebuild friendships. You may feel:

- Emotionally exhausted.
- Unsure of who to trust.

- Misunderstood by those who didn't walk through your storm.
- Afraid of becoming vulnerable again.

But healing thrives in a safe community.

You don't need a crowd—just a few who love you authentically, call you higher, and walk beside you without judgment. Ask God to send divine connections—*those who match your healed pace, not your broken history.*

FAMILY DYNAMICS AFTER SURVIVAL

Let's talk honestly: some of the deepest wounds come from family. And sometimes, the healing journey requires redefining or even releasing certain family dynamics to preserve your peace.

Living beyond survival doesn't mean you have to stay in toxic cycles just because someone shares your bloodline.

Honor does not require access. Forgiveness does not mean enabling.

You can love people from a distance. You can set limits. You can create new boundaries. And you can choose to protect your emotional and spiritual health without guilt.

Jesus said in Matthew 12:50, *"Anyone who does the will of my Father in heaven is my brother and sister and mother!" (NLT).*

He understood that **kingdom relationships sometimes supersede biological ones**.

ROMANTIC RELATIONSHIPS BEYOND SURVIVAL

Romantic love often suffers the most under the weight of unhealed trauma.

You may find yourself:

- Distrusting someone who has done nothing wrong.
- Needing constant reassurance.
- Withdrawing when things get too real.
- Expecting abandonment or betrayal.
- Losing yourself in the relationship to feel valuable.

But the relationship that's built on fear will eventually collapse under the pressure.

You must heal first—for you. Not just so you can be a "better partner," but so you can show up whole, confident, secure, and emotionally free.

A healthy relationship is not your *rescue*—it's your *reward*. And it must be stewarded with intention, not desperation.

HOW TO BUILD HEALTHY, HEALED RELATIONSHIPS

1. Be honest about where you are.

Don't hide your story—share it with people who have earned your trust.

2. Communicate openly.

Don't expect people to guess your needs. Speak in truth and love.

3. Set clear boundaries.

Decide ahead of time what's acceptable—and what's not.

4. Choose healing over proving.

You don't have to defend how much you've changed. Let your peace prove it.

5. Allow God to lead your relationships.

Don't cling to people out of history or comfort. Ask, *"Does this relationship align with who I'm becoming?"*

YOU DESERVE REAL LOVE—NOT JUST LOYALTY IN PAIN

Loyalty is good—but don't confuse loyalty with alignment.

Some people are loyal to your *wounds*—not your *wellness*.

As you heal, your relationships will shift. That's okay. Let what needs to fall away, fall.

Let those who need to exit, exit.

God will send what's aligned with your assignment.

You are not too much.
You are not too broken.
You are not too late.
You are becoming the healed version of yourself—and the relationships you build now will reflect that healing.

SCRIPTURES FOR REFLECTION

And the Lord God said, It is not good that the man should be alone; I will make him an help meet for him. —Genesis 2:18

Beareth all things, believeth all things, hopeth all things, endureth all things. —1 Corinthians 13:7

For whosoever shall do the will of my Father which is in heaven, the same is my brother, and sister, and mother. —Matthew 12:50

He that walketh with wise men shall be wise: but a companion of fools shall be destroyed. —Proverbs 13:20

Two are better than one; because they have a good reward for their labour. For if they fall, the one will lift up his fellow: but woe to him that is alone when he falleth; for he hath not another to help him up. —Ecclesiastes 4:9–10

Can two walk together, except they be agreed? —Amos 3:3

DECLARATION

I am worthy of healthy relationships. I release toxic connections, people-pleasing patterns, and emotional fear. I walk in love, truth, and discernment. I am attracting relationships that reflect my healing, not my history. I honor myself and others by communicating with clarity and living with peace. I am free to love, and I am loved in return.

CHAPTER 14

RECLAIMING DREAMS AND DESIRES

One of the greatest casualties of survival mode isn't just your peace—it's your **dreams**.

When life becomes about making it through the day, you lose the luxury of imagination. Dreams feel unrealistic. Desires feel dangerous. And slowly, without even realizing it, you stop hoping for more. You silence your creativity. You mute your voice. You bury your longing.

But God never intended for your purpose to die in the pit of pain.

What survival buried, healing can resurrect.

It's time to reclaim your dreams. To rediscover what makes you come alive. To believe again. To desire again. Not out of desperation, but out of the deep assurance that you were *created* to thrive—not just endure.

SURVIVAL TEACHES YOU TO SETTLE

When your energy is spent on staying afloat, you stop reaching for anything that looks like risk.

You settle for:

- Jobs that pay the bills but drain your soul.
- Relationships that are safe but not nourishing.
- Routines that are predictable but not fulfilling.
- Dreams that are small enough not to scare you.

You tell yourself, "At least I'm not where I used to be."

And while gratitude is powerful, stagnation is not sanctified.

God didn't bring you through the storm just to leave you sitting in survival's shadow.

He brought you out to build something new. Something bold. Something beautiful.

THE POWER OF DREAMS

Dreams are more than random ideas or passing thoughts. They are *divine deposits*—glimpses of what could be, seeded by the Spirit.

Proverbs 13:12: *"Hope deferred makes the heart sick, but a longing fulfilled is a tree of life." (NIV).*

When you stop dreaming, your heart begins to die in slow, silent ways.

- You stop imagining better.
- You stop praying with boldness.
- You stop expecting God to do more than what you've seen before.

But you were created with divine imagination. You carry within you blueprints for books, businesses, ministries, art, songs, strategies, and systems. And it's time to dig those dreams out of the grave.

GOD HONORS HOLY DESIRE

There is a lie that says wanting more makes you ungrateful. That dreaming bigger makes you prideful. That desire is dangerous.

But here's the truth: when your desires are submitted to God, they become sacred.

Psalm 37:4: *"Take delight in the Lord, and He will give you the desires of your heart." (NIV).*

This doesn't mean God is your genie. It means when you're aligned with Him, He shapes your desires—and fulfills them in ways that bring glory to His name and joy to your soul.

Don't demonize your dreams. Don't minimize your vision.

Desire isn't your enemy—it's often your compass.

HOW TO RECLAIM THE DREAMS YOU LOST

1. Acknowledge the Dreams You Buried

What did you once believe in before the pain? Before fear took over?

2. Write Them Down Without Judgment

Don't filter your vision through logic or past disappointment. Just let it flow.

3. Ask God for Clarity

Invite the Holy Spirit to breathe life and direction into your dreams.

4. Take One Brave Step

You don't need to leap—you just need to *move*. Make the call. Write the outline. Say yes.

5. Surround Yourself with Vision-Driven Voices

Your environment matters. Be around those who speak life into your dreams—not death.

WHEN DREAMS SEEM DELAYED

Let's be honest—some dreams feel delayed for *years*. You start to wonder:

- Did I miss God?
- Did I wait too long?
- Did I blow my chance?

But delay is not denial.

Habakkuk 2:3: *"This vision is for a future time. It describes the end, and it will be fulfilled. If it seems slow in coming, wait patiently, for it will surely take place. It will not be delayed." (NLT).*

God is not in a rush. He's in the business of **perfect timing**. Some dreams require development—*not just of the dream, but of the dreamer.*

While you've been healing, God's been preparing. While you've been waiting, God's been aligning. He hasn't forgotten your vision—He's been refining it.

YOUR DREAMS STILL MATTER

Even the ones you shelved.
Even the ones people mocked.
Even the ones you stopped praying about.
Even the ones that felt "too late."

God doesn't waste dreams. He doesn't forget blueprints. He doesn't cancel assignments.

If He gave you the vision, He's also given you the *grace* to see it fulfilled.

This is your season to reclaim it.

FROM DREAMING TO BUILDING

Once you reclaim your dream, you must also be willing to *build it.*

That means:

Pastor Dr. Claudine Benjamin

- Planning with strategy.
- Working with discipline.
- Enduring through discouragement.
- Trusting God with timing.
- Remaining consistent when no one's watching.

God gives the vision—but He also expects *your participation.*

James 2:17: *"So you see, faith by itself isn't enough. Unless it produces good deeds, it is dead and useless." (NLT).*

Faith dreams it.
Obedience builds it.

YOU ARE NOT TOO LATE

This lie must die today: *"I missed my moment."*

No. You're right on time.

Because the healed version of you is *ready* to carry what the wounded version could not.
You are not too old.
You are not too broken.
You are not too inexperienced.
You are *called, equipped, anointed,* and *ready.*

SCRIPTURES FOR REFLECTION

Hope deferred maketh the heart sick: but when the desire cometh, it is a tree of life. —Proverbs 13:12

Delight thyself also in the Lord: and he shall give thee the desires of thine heart. —Psalm 37:4

For the vision is yet for an appointed time, but at the end it shall speak, and not lie: though it tarry, wait for it; because it will surely come, it will not tarry. —Habakkuk 2:3

And I will restore to you the years that the locust hath eaten, the cankerworm, and the caterpiller, and the palmerworm, my great army which I sent among you. —Joel 2:25

For I know the thoughts that I think toward you, saith the Lord, thoughts of peace, and not of evil, to give you an expected end. — Jeremiah 29:11

Now unto him that is able to do exceeding abundantly above all that we ask or think, according to the power that worketh in us, — Ephesians 3:20

DECLARATION

I reclaim every dream I buried. I no longer fear disappointment or delay. I believe that what God planted in me still matters. I am aligned with purpose, filled with holy desire, and ready to take the next step. I will not shrink. I will not settle. I will build. I will believe. I will dream again—with boldness, faith, and joy.

CHAPTER 15

THE FAITH TO LIVE AGAIN

There's a special kind of faith required not to be healed—but to **live again**.

It's one thing to survive the storm. It's another thing to **believe again after the storm has passed**. To believe that laughter will return. That love can be real. That joy can be sustained. That peace isn't a tease. That purpose still belongs to you.

This chapter is for those who've stood at the edge of hope and hesitated.

You've seen too much. Lost too much. Felt too much.

But now, the invitation is clear: **It's time to rise. It's time to believe again. It's time to live.**

FAITH ISN'T JUST FOR CRISIS—IT'S FOR WHOLENESS

Many of us learned how to activate faith in the fire. We know how to pray when everything's falling apart. We know how to cry out in desperation. We know how to believe for survival.

But now—God is calling you to **believe for more** than just rescue.

He wants to teach you how to have **faith for abundance**.
Faith for consistency.
Faith for joy.
Faith for laughter.
Faith for the simple, beautiful days.
Faith not just to *make it*—but to *maintain it*.

Mark 5:34: *"Daughter, your faith has healed you. Go in peace and be freed from your suffering." (NIV)*.

It wasn't just about healing. It was about *living again*, in peace and freedom.

FAITH TO LIVE AGAIN REQUIRES RISK

Living again means stepping out without guarantees. It means:

- Opening your heart after heartbreak.
- Starting over after failure.
- Dreaming again after disappointment.
- Trusting again after betrayal.
- Laughing again after loss.

This kind of faith is *raw*. It's not polished. It trembles sometimes. It has flashbacks. It whispers, *"What if it happens again?"*

But it also dares to hope.

It says, *"Even if it happens again, I'll survive—and this time, I'll thrive."*

FAITH IN THE GOD OF THE COMEBACK

The Bible is full of comeback stories powered by faith:

- **Job** lost everything—and God restored double.
- **Naomi** said, "Call me bitter"—but became the grandmother of royalty.
- **David** sinned, suffered, and still sang.
- **Peter** denied Christ—but preached the gospel to thousands.
- **Jesus** was buried—and rose again in glory.

God is a God of restoration, redemption, and resurrection. He doesn't just bring people out—**He brings them back stronger**.

Joel 2:25: *"I will repay you for the years the locusts have eaten—" (NIV)*.

You haven't missed your moment. You're standing at the edge of a **comeback**. But it requires one thing: **faith to live again.**

SIGNS YOUR FAITH IS WAKING UP

- You start imagining new possibilities.
- You feel a strange mix of fear and excitement.
- You catch yourself smiling more, crying less.
- You begin to respond to life instead of reacting to trauma.
- You start to hope—even if it scares you.

These are not signs of foolishness. These are signs of **faith**.

Faith is the evidence of things not yet seen. You may not see it clearly—but if you're feeling the stir, *God is already working*.

FAITH AFTER DISAPPOINTMENT

Let's pause and be real: disappointment is dangerous. It steals faith. It builds walls. It creates inner vows like:

- "I'll never trust again."
- "I'll never try again."
- "I'll never get my hopes up."

But those walls don't protect you. They *trap you.*

Faith is the courage to say, *"Even though I was disappointed before, I will trust God again."*

Not because you understand everything, but because you trust **His nature**.

Lamentations 3:22–23: *"Because of the Lord's great love we are not consumed, for his compassions never fail. They are new every morning; great is your faithfulness." (NIV).*

Every sunrise is an invitation to live again.

FAITH MOVES YOU INTO ACTION

Faith is not just a feeling—it's a *force*. And it moves.

- Faith gets out of the bed when depression says, "Stay down."
- Faith goes on the job interview even after the last no.
- Faith writes the book, applies to school, forgives the past, opens the heart, sends the message, and signs the lease.
- Faith walks—even if it's limping.

James 2:17: *"Faith by itself, if it is not accompanied by action, is dead." (NIV).*

You don't need a 5-year plan. You just need to take one brave step—and let God meet you in the movement.

GIVE YOURSELF PERMISSION TO LIVE

This might be the hardest part.

You've carried pain so long, joy feels like betrayal.
You've cried so much, laughter feels out of place.
You've grieved so deeply, peace feels suspicious.

But hear this in your spirit: **You are allowed to live.**

You are allowed to be happy.
You are allowed to dream again.
You are allowed to love.
You are allowed to enjoy your life—even as you honor what you've been through.

Living again is not betrayal of the past. It's the fulfillment of God's promise to bring **beauty from ashes**.

YOUR STORY ISN'T OVER

Not only is it not over—it's just getting started.

The healed you.
The joyful you.
The bold you.

The fulfilled you.
The present, hopeful, expectant you.
Faith is your fuel.
Hope is your compass.
Love is your foundation.
And **God is your strength.**
You've survived long enough.
Now—**live.**

SCRIPTURES FOR REFLECTION

And he said unto her, Daughter, thy faith hath made thee whole; go in peace, and be whole of thy plague. —Mark 5:34

And I will restore to you the years that the locust hath eaten, the cankerworm, and the caterpiller, and the palmerworm, my great army which I sent among you. —Joel 2:25

It is of the Lord's mercies that we are not consumed, because his compassions fail not. They are new every morning: great is thy faithfulness. —Lamentations 3:22–23

Even so faith, if it hath not works, is dead, being alone. —James 2:17

I had fainted, unless I had believed to see the goodness of the Lord in the land of the living. —Psalm 27:13

Now faith is the substance of things hoped for, the evidence of things not seen. —Hebrews 11:1

DECLARATION

I have the faith to live again. I release fear, regret, and disappointment. I choose hope. I choose joy. I choose forward movement. I declare that my best days are not behind me—they are ahead. I am no longer surviving—I am living, with boldness, peace, and unwavering faith in the God who restores, revives, and makes all things new.

CHAPTER 16

LEAVING EGYPT, EMBRACING CANAAN

Y ou've cried.
     You've endured.
     You've rebuilt.
You've survived.

But survival was never meant to be your final destination.

There comes a moment when you must leave **Egypt**—the place of bondage, limitation, trauma, and slavery to fear—and embrace **Canaan**—the land of promise, purpose, and overflow.

This chapter is a call to **transition**. Not just geographically, but **mentally, emotionally, spiritually, and relationally**. You're leaving the place that broke you and entering the place God designed to **bless you**.

And no—this transition isn't easy. But it is necessary.

EGYPT: THE PLACE OF SURVIVAL

Egypt represents:

- The systems that enslaved you.
- The cycles that wore you down.
- The people who never saw your value.
- The mindset that made you play small.
- The fear that kept you still.

You didn't choose Egypt—but you survived it. And sometimes, even after deliverance, **Egypt remains in your mind.**

Just like the Israelites, who were physically free but emotionally bound, you may still be looking back:

- Longing for what was familiar, even if it was dysfunctional.
- Doubting whether you're truly free.
- Craving control because the wilderness feels uncertain.

Exodus 16:3: *"If only we had died by the Lord's hand in Egypt! There we sat around pots of meat…" (NIV).*

They were out—but they still remembered bondage as comfort. Because survival, as toxic as it is, can become comfortable.

CANAAN: THE LAND OF PROMISE

Canaan represents:

- Fulfilled promises
- New identity
- New responsibilities
- Overflow, inheritance, and fruitfulness
- The place where the **vision comes alive**

But Canaan also requires **courage**. Because before you enter the promise, you must face:

- The **giants** of fear and insecurity.
- The **fortified walls** of old thought patterns.
- The **unknowns** of a land you've never walked before.

You cannot take Egypt's mindset into Canaan's territory.

You must shift from being a **slave of survival** to a **steward of promise.**

CROSSING OVER REQUIRES A DECISION

The Jordan River represents the line between **what was** and **what will be**.

When Joshua led the people into Canaan, it wasn't just a geographical shift—it was a spiritual moment of **alignment and obedience**.

Joshua 3:5: *"Consecrate yourselves, for tomorrow the Lord will do amazing things among you." (NIV).*

God is calling you to:

- Set yourself apart.
- Let go of what no longer serves your future.
- Prepare your heart to receive more.
- Believe that what's ahead is *better* than what's behind.

WHY SOME NEVER ENTER CANAAN

Sadly, not everyone who left Egypt made it to Canaan.

Why? Because they:

- Complained more than they trusted.
- Refused to release old mindsets.
- Rebelled against God's instructions.
- Let fear rule their decisions.
- Focused on giants instead of God's power.

Numbers 13:33b: *"We seemed like grasshoppers in our own eyes, and we looked the same to them." (NIV).*

Your view of yourself matters.
You will not conquer what you don't believe you're equipped for.

God says you're more than a conqueror. That settles it.

EMBRACING THE NEW REQUIRES SHEDDING THE OLD

Before they entered the promised land, Joshua had to **circumcise** a new generation. It was symbolic—a cutting away of what was holding them back.

Joshua 5:9: *"Today I have rolled away the reproach of Egypt from you." (NIV).*

That reproach may be:

- The shame of what happened to you.

- The regret of your past choices.
- The residue of people's opinions.
- The bitterness that lingered in silence.

Let it go.
Canaan can't coexist with Egypt's baggage.

THE PROMISE REQUIRES PARTICIPATION

Yes, Canaan is promised.
But it's not handed to you on a silver platter.

You must still:

- Fight battles
- Follow strategy
- Stay faithful
- Walk in obedience

But the difference now? **God goes before you.**

You're not just trying to survive. You're stepping into a season where **He fights for you, blesses you, and establishes you.**

WHAT LIVING IN CANAAN LOOKS LIKE

- Your decisions come from identity, not insecurity.
- Your prayers are bolder and less apologetic.
- You dream with confidence.
- You rest without guilt.
- You build with intentionality.
- You no longer flinch at good things—*you receive them.*

121

CANAAN IS NOT PERFECTION—IT'S PROMISE FULFILLED

You will still face challenges. But this time, you know who you are.
You're not the same person who cried in Egypt.
You're stronger. Wiser. Healed. Prepared.

THIS IS YOUR CROSSOVER MOMENT

You don't have to know every detail.
You just have to step.
God is already clearing the way.
The manna may have stopped—but the harvest is *waiting.*
Leave Egypt.
Say goodbye to survival.
And walk boldly into the life that's been waiting for you.

SCRIPTURES FOR REFLECTION

And the children of Israel said unto them, would to God we had died by the hand of the Lord in the land of Egypt, when we sat by the flesh pots, and when we did eat bread to the full; for ye have brought us forth into this wilderness, to kill this whole assembly with hunger. —Exodus 16:3

And there we saw the giants, the sons of Anak, which come of the giants: and we were in our own sight as grasshoppers, and so we were in their sight. —Numbers 13:33

And Joshua said unto the people, Sanctify yourselves: for to morrow the Lord will do wonders among you. —Joshua 3:5

And the Lord said unto Joshua, This day have I rolled away the reproach of Egypt from off you. Wherefore the name of the place is called Gilgal unto this day. —Joshua 5:9

The Lord our God spake unto us in Horeb, saying, Ye have dwelt long enough in this mount: —Deuteronomy 1:6

Remember ye not the former things, neither consider the things of old. Behold, I will do a new thing; now it shall spring forth; shall ye not know it? I will even make a way in the wilderness, and rivers in the desert. —Isaiah 43:18–19

DECLARATION

I am leaving Egypt for good. I let go of trauma, fear, and every lie that kept me small. I will not romanticize my pain. I will not return to what God has delivered me from. I embrace Canaan. I receive promise, provision, and purpose. I walk by faith. I move with boldness. I live in the land of God's favor—and I will never go back.

CHAPTER 17

BUILDING A LIFE WORTH LIVING

N ow that you've left survival behind, it's time to build.

Not just a schedule.

Not just a routine.

Not just an income.

But a **life**—a life that reflects the healing, freedom, and purpose God has deposited in you.

This isn't about filling your calendar with activities or chasing worldly success. This is about **intentionally designing a life that aligns with God's promises, honors your journey, and brings joy to your soul**.

You've survived the storm. You've crossed over from Egypt. You've started healing. Now it's time to lay the bricks of the future.

WHAT MAKES A LIFE WORTH LIVING?

It's not measured by status or material things. A life worth living is rooted in:

- **Purpose**: Knowing why you're here.
- **Peace**: Guarding your internal atmosphere.
- **Presence**: Being fully engaged in the now.
- **People**: Loving and being loved well.
- **Passion**: Doing what lights your spirit.
- **Praise**: Giving glory to God in every season.

Jesus didn't say, "I came so they could barely make it."

He said, *"I came that they might have life, and have it to the full"* (see John 10:10).

A full life is a **balanced** life—filled with meaning, not just movement.

LIFE AFTER SURVIVAL REQUIRES INTENTION

When you've been in survival mode, life can feel reactive. You only respond to emergencies. You make decisions from fear. You avoid taking risks.

But now, you're being called to **intentionality**.

You don't stumble into a life worth living—you **build it on purpose**.

- You cultivate joy.
- You protect your time.
- You invest in what matters.
- You say yes to growth and no to drama.
- You dream with structure and act with discipline.

This is what spiritual maturity looks like: not just freedom from chaos, but responsibility with freedom.

FOUNDATIONS THAT LAST

Matthew 7:24: *"Therefore everyone who hears these words of mine and puts them into practice is like a wise man who built his house on the rock." (NIV).*

If you want to build a life that lasts, you must start with the right foundation.

That means:

- Building on **God's truth**, not emotions.
- Anchoring your identity in **Christ**, not people's opinions.
- Building rhythms of **rest, prayer, and study.**
- Refusing to compromise values for validation.
- Living by **conviction**, not comparison.

The storms may come again—but this time, your house will *stand.*

WHAT DO YOU WANT THIS LIFE TO LOOK LIKE?

Ask yourself:

- What do I want to be known for?
- What makes me feel fully alive?
- What brings peace into my space?
- Who do I want to be surrounded by?
- How do I want to spend my time?

This is not selfish. This is stewardship.

You get one life on this side of eternity. And God has entrusted you with time, gifts, influence, and wisdom. Use them well.

You're not here to merely exist. You're here to **build a life that glorifies God and nourishes your soul.**

BUILD SLOWLY, BUILD WISELY

Don't rush.
Don't compare your progress.
Don't build on borrowed blueprints.

This is *your* life. Your assignment. Your pace. Your path.

Some days you'll build with confidence. Other days, with trembling hands. That's okay. Just keep building.

Zechariah 4:10: *"Do not despise these small beginnings, for the Lord rejoices to see the work begin…" (NLT).*

One habit.
One prayer.
One boundary.
One conversation.
One courageous "yes" at a time.

INCLUDE GOD IN THE BLUEPRINT

Before you build anything—invite the Master Architect.

Psalm 127:1: *"Unless the Lord builds the house, the builders labor in vain." (NIV).*

Let God help you:

- Design your daily life.
- Discern your priorities.
- Decide what to release and what to embrace.
- Detect distractions.
- Develop habits of health and holiness.

When God builds with you, your life won't just stand—it will **flourish**.

YOUR FUTURE DESERVES YOUR PARTICIPATION

You've prayed for it.
You've cried for it.
Now it's time to **co-labor** with God and participate in the life you asked Him for.

This means:

- Showing up with intention.
- Making decisions that align with your destiny.
- Saying no to what no longer serves your future.
- Walking by faith even when fear whispers louder.

You're not just reacting anymore—you're **creating**.
You're not stuck—you're **strategic**.
You're not lost—you're **led**.

Pastor Dr. Claudine Benjamin

A LIFE WORTH LIVING IS A LIFE WORTH PROTECTING

As you build:

- Guard your peace.
- Water your joy.
- Weed out drama.
- Make room for fun.
- Stay humble, but honor your growth.
- Don't downplay your progress.

You've been through enough. This next season is about building what **reflects your healing**, not your hurt.

You are no longer rebuilding ruins—you are **raising legacy.**

SCRIPTURES FOR REFLECTION

The thief cometh not, but for to steal, and to kill, and to destroy: I am come that they might have life, and that they might have it more abundantly. —John 10:10

Therefore whosoever heareth these sayings of mine, and doeth them, I will liken him unto a wise man, which built his house upon a rock: And the rain descended, and the floods came, and the winds blew, and beat upon that house; and it fell not: for it was founded upon a rock. —Matthew 7:24–25

Except the Lord build the house, they labour in vain that build it: except the Lord keep the city, the watchman waketh but in vain. — Psalm 127:1

For who hath despised the day of small things? for they shall rejoice, and shall see the plummet in the hand of Zerubbabel with those seven; they are the eyes of the Lord, which run to and fro through the whole earth. —Zechariah 4:10

And they shall build the old wastes, they shall raise up the former desolations, and they shall repair the waste cities, the desolations of many generations. —Isaiah 61:4

Through wisdom is an house builded; and by understanding it is established: —Proverbs 24:3

DECLARATION

I am building a life worth living. I release chaos, confusion, and meaningless motion. I build on God's truth, with wisdom and peace. I am intentional, disciplined, and full of joy. My life reflects healing. My future is bright. My faith is strong. I will live with purpose, and I will build with power—brick by brick, and step by step.

CHAPTER 18

THE POWER OF GRATITUDE AND PRESENCE

When you've lived in survival mode, your attention is constantly pulled into the past (what hurt you) or projected into the future (what might go wrong). The present becomes blurry, overlooked, or even feared.

But true freedom is found not just in healing the past or preparing for the future—it's in learning to be **fully present** and deeply **grateful** in the *now*.

Gratitude and presence are not emotional luxuries. They are spiritual disciplines.

They are how we stop surviving and start truly **living**.

SURVIVAL MODE MAKES YOU DISTRACTED AND DISCONNECTED

In survival mode:

- You struggle to enjoy the moment because you're waiting for something bad to happen.
- You obsess over what didn't work or worry about what's coming next.
- You downplay good things, expecting them to disappear.
- You live busy, but not *present.*

And what you miss in the process is **life itself**.

Life isn't lived in the regrets of yesterday or the fears of tomorrow. It is lived in the sacred space of *right now.*

GRATITUDE SHIFTS THE ATMOSPHERE

Gratitude isn't just saying thank you—it's **training your spirit to see God at work**, even in the small things.

1 Thessalonians 5:18: *"Give thanks in all circumstances; for this is God's will for you in Christ Jesus." (NIV).*

Notice it doesn't say to give thanks *for* everything—but to give thanks *in* everything.

That means:

- In progress, be thankful.
- In waiting, be thankful.
- In transition, be thankful.
- In healing, be thankful.

Gratitude doesn't ignore pain—it anchors you in **perspective**.

THE SCIENCE AND SPIRIT OF GRATITUDE

Even science confirms what Scripture already says: Gratitude rewires your brain. It reduces anxiety, combats depression, increases joy, and promotes better sleep and overall well-being.

But spiritually, gratitude is even more powerful. It:

- Invites the presence of God (see Psalm 100:4).
- Unlocks contentment (see Philippians 4:11–13).
- Defeats bitterness.
- Guards your heart from entitlement.
- Prepares you for increase.

Gratitude attracts abundance because God can trust a grateful heart to steward blessings well.

PRESENCE IS A FORM OF WORSHIP

God doesn't just want you to look forward to heaven—He wants you to *live fully here.*

Psalm 118:24: *"The Lord has done it this very day; let us rejoice today and be glad." (NIV).*

Not tomorrow.
Not once the healing is complete.
Not once the bills are paid.
Not once the dream is fulfilled.

This is the day. And if you're breathing, *you're already blessed.*

Presence says:

- I will enjoy this meal.
- I will laugh without guilt.
- I will put the phone down and soak in my child's laughter.
- I will thank God even if nothing changes today—because He is still good.

THE ENEMY WANTS TO STEAL TODAY

The devil can't undo your salvation, but he'll do everything to rob your **satisfaction**—and one of his main strategies is distraction.

He'll keep you so worried about tomorrow that you miss today's blessings.

He'll keep you so focused on what you don't have that you overlook what's right in front of you.

But your best defense is simple: **grateful presence**.

You win by being fully aware of God's goodness, right here, right now.

HOW TO PRACTICE GRATITUDE AND PRESENCE DAILY

1. **Start your day with thanks**

Before you check your phone, check in with your soul. What are three things you're thankful for?

2. **Pause to observe**

Look for the beauty in the ordinary—sunlight, a kind smile, your breath.

3. **Limit digital distractions**

Set boundaries around your time and attention. You can't be fully present if you're always plugged in elsewhere.

4. **Keep a gratitude journal**

Write down small victories, answered prayers, and moments that warmed your heart.

5. **Use breath prayers or scripture reminders**

Center yourself throughout the day with verses like: *"Be still and know..."* (see Psalm 46:10).

GRATITUDE FUELS CONTENTMENT WITHOUT KILLING VISION

Gratitude doesn't mean settling. You can still dream for more, build for better, and grow in faith—*while loving where you are.*

It's not either/or. It's *both.*

You can be fully content in your present while trusting God for your future.

You can praise in the hallway while the door is still closed.

Pastor Dr. Claudine Benjamin

Because **living with gratitude and presence means you've matured in your faith.**

YOU'RE NOT BEHIND—YOU'RE ALIVE

So many people live rushing toward the next season because they believe *this* one isn't enough.
But don't miss the gift of **now**.

You're alive.
You're healing.
You're growing.
You're surrounded by miracles in disguise.

Slow down. Look around. Take it in.

SCRIPTURES FOR REFLECTION

In every thing give thanks: for this is the will of God in Christ Jesus concerning you. —1 Thessalonians 5:18

This is the day which the Lord hath made; we will rejoice and be glad in it. —Psalm 118:24

Not that I speak in respect of want: for I have learned, in whatsoever state I am, therewith to be content. I know both how to be abased, and I know how to abound: every where and in all things I am instructed both to be full and to be hungry, both to abound and to suffer need. I can do all things through Christ which strengtheneth me. —Philippians 4:11–13

Enter into his gates with thanksgiving, and into his courts with praise: be thankful unto him, and bless his name. —Psalm 100:4

It is of the Lord's mercies that we are not consumed, because his compassions fail not. They are new every morning: great is thy faithfulness. —Lamentations 3:22–23

And also that every man should eat and drink, and enjoy the good of all his labour, it is the gift of God. —Ecclesiastes 3:13

DECLARATION

I live with gratitude and presence. I am not bound by yesterday or anxious about tomorrow. I see God's goodness here, now, today. I give thanks in all things. I protect my peace. I choose joy in the simple moments. I will not miss my life rushing through it—I will slow down, give thanks, and live deeply. Today is a gift, and I receive it fully.

CHAPTER 19

LIVING FULLY IN EVERY SEASON

Real freedom isn't just found in healing—it's found in the ability to **live fully in every season**, whether it's a time of sunshine or shadow, momentum or stillness, abundance or pruning.

The goal of this journey is not to finally reach a perfect, pain-free life. The goal is to become so rooted in God's presence, truth, and identity that you can flourish no matter what season you're in.

You don't just want a life that functions when everything's good. You want a life that **thrives in all conditions**—a life built on faith, anchored in peace, and fueled by purpose, even when the scenery shifts.

LIFE COMES IN SEASONS

Ecclesiastes 3:1: *"There is a time for everything, and a season for every activity under the heavens:" (NIV).*

Just like nature, your life will go through:

Pastor Dr. Claudine Benjamin

- Seasons of **growth** (spring).
- Seasons of **productivity** (summer).
- Seasons of **transition** (autumn).
- Seasons of **rest or waiting** (winter).

Each one has value. Each one has purpose.
And each one requires a different kind of faith.

Living fully means **not resisting the season**, but learning from it.

It means showing up *completely present*, even when things don't look how you expected.

DON'T RUSH THROUGH THE SEASON YOU'RE IN

We often want to escape hard seasons—rush through the waiting, skip the quiet, bypass the stretching. But doing so robs us of what the season was sent to produce.

Ask yourself:

- What is this season teaching me?
- What fruit is God developing in me?
- What part of me is being strengthened?
- What should I let go of to make room for what's next?

Romans 5:3-4: *"suffering produces perseverance; perseverance, character; and character, hope." (NIV).*

Every season builds something in you.

And when you allow God to work in you fully, you'll look back and see that nothing was wasted.

LIVING FULLY MEANS LIVING AWAKE

Many people sleepwalk through their seasons. They numb out. Check out. Distract themselves with busyness, entertainment, or shallow relationships.

But when you live *awake*—spiritually, emotionally, mentally—you become deeply aware of:

- God's hand in the process.
- The lessons hidden in every moment.
- The quiet joy of slow growth.
- The people you're called to pour into (or be poured into by).

Colossians 4:5: *"Live wisely among those who are not believers, and make the most of every opportunity." (NLT).*

Your season is not random.
And your presence in it is not accidental.

HOW TO LIVE FULLY IN EACH TYPE OF SEASON

In a Season of Growth (Spring)
- Be open to change.
- Embrace new opportunities.
- Say yes to stretching.
- Guard your roots while reaching for more.

In a Season of Productivity (Summer)

- Steward your energy wisely.
- Stay focused—don't burn out.
- Celebrate the wins.
- Sow seeds that will feed you in winter.

In a Season of Transition (Autumn)

- Let go of what no longer fits.
- Reflect without regret.
- Prepare for change.
- Trust that the shedding is necessary.

In a Season of Waiting or Rest (Winter)

- Slow down without guilt.
- Nourish your soul.
- Listen more than you speak.
- Remember that rest is *not* inactivity—it's **preparation.**

DON'T COMPARE YOUR SEASON TO SOMEONE ELSE'S

One of the greatest threats to living fully is **comparison**. You'll always feel behind when you compare your winter to someone else's summer.

You're not late.
You're not forgotten.
You're not less faithful just because your life looks slower.
Trust God's **timeline** for you.
He's cultivating you uniquely, for a purpose greater than what you can see right now.

EVERY SEASON HAS A SONG

Even David, a man after God's own heart, wrote songs from **every place**:

- From the palace *and* the pasture.
- From the cave *and* the throne.
- From the battlefield *and* the secret place.

He learned to worship in all seasons.
Can you?
Can you praise when you don't understand?
Can you sing when you're sowing in tears?

This is how you live fully—*by anchoring your heart in God, not in your surroundings.*

SIGNS YOU'RE LIVING FULLY

- You wake up with gratitude, not dread.
- You stop asking "Why me?" and start asking "What now?"
- You create beauty in ordinary moments.
- You let yourself feel deeply.
- You surrender without giving up.
- You serve without striving.
- You trust without seeing everything.

Living fully isn't about pretending it's always good—it's about trusting that **God is good** in every moment.

SCRIPTURES FOR REFLECTION

To every thing there is a season, and a time to every purpose under the heaven: —Ecclesiastes 3:1

And not only so, but we glory in tribulations also: knowing that tribulation worketh patience; And patience, experience; and experience, hope: —Romans 5:3–4

Walk in wisdom toward them that are without, redeeming the time. —Colossians 4:5

And he shall be like a tree planted by the rivers of water, that bringeth forth his fruit in his season; his leaf also shall not wither; and whatsoever he doeth shall prosper. —Psalm 1:3

And let us not be weary in well doing: for in due season we shall reap, if we faint not. —Galatians 6:9

But they that wait upon the Lord shall renew their strength; they shall mount up with wings as eagles; they shall run, and not be weary; and they shall walk, and not faint. —Isaiah 40:31

DECLARATION

I live fully in every season. I do not rush what God is doing. I do not compare my path to others. I embrace the beauty, lessons, and growth in every stage of my life. I remain rooted, grateful, and present. I am awake to God's hand at work in me. No season is wasted. My life is fruitful in every phase—and I live it fully, boldly, and with purpose.

CHAPTER 20

IT'S YOUR TIME TO THRIVE

You've survived the storm.

You've crossed the wilderness.

You've faced the pain, done the healing, reclaimed your voice, and begun to dream again.

But now, it's time for something more.

Not just survival. Not just stability. Not just small wins.
It's time to **thrive**.

Thriving isn't about perfection. It's about flourishing.

It's about becoming everything God had in mind when He created you.

It's about moving forward, not just healed—but *whole, bold, and unstoppable.*

WHAT DOES THRIVING ACTUALLY MEAN?

To thrive means to:

- **Grow** in strength, peace, and wisdom.
- **Flourish** in your faith, purpose, and relationships.
- **Shine** without apology or shrinking.
- **Produce fruit**—in every area of life.
- **Walk in freedom**—consistently and confidently.

Thriving isn't loud or showy. It's a quiet confidence. A rooted life. A radiant spirit.
It's waking up with peace and going to sleep with purpose.
It's not just about what you achieve—but about **who you become**.

THRIVING IS YOUR BIRTHRIGHT IN CHRIST

John 15:5: *"I am the vine; you are the branches. If you remain in me and I in you, you will bear much fruit…" (NIV).*

You were created to bear fruit—**good fruit**.
Not anxiety, fear, or endless hustle. But peace, love, clarity, confidence, and impact.
God's plan for you has always been more than survival.
Even in Genesis, the first command God gave humanity was to **be fruitful and multiply**.

This means:

- There's more for you to discover.
- More for you to create.
- More for you to impact.
- More for you to experience in Christ.

WHAT THRIVING IS *NOT*

Let's be clear—thriving doesn't mean:

- You never struggle.
- You never feel pain.
- You always have it together.
- You become too busy to prove your growth.

THRIVING IS NOT PERFORMANCE, IT'S POSTURE

It's how you position your heart.
It's how you respond to pressure.
It's how you hold on to truth when the lies try to rise up.
It's how you remain *planted* when others are chasing applause.

YOUR THRIVE SEASON LOOKS LIKE

- Peace that makes no sense.
- Boundaries that honor your healing.
- Relationships that reflect your growth.
- Bold prayers and big dreams.
- Obedience without compromise.
- Joy without fear of loss.
- Progress without apology.

You're not just managing anymore. You're **mastering** the life God gave you. You're not afraid of "too much." You've decided that you are worthy of **overflow**.

BARRIERS THAT BLOCK THRIVING

Even now, the enemy would love to keep you from thriving. Not because you can't—but because he's afraid of what your thriving will unleash.

Here are a few common blockers:

- **Guilt** over outgrowing people or spaces.
- **Fear** that good things won't last.
- **Imposter syndrome** that says you don't belong in this level of peace.
- **Perfectionism** that stalls your forward movement.
- **Comparison** that keeps you distracted.

But guess what?

You can break every one of those with **truth**.

God does not elevate you into thriving so you can shrink back—He does it so you can **shine forward**.

YOU'RE NOT JUST THRIVING FOR YOU

Your healing was personal.
Your breakthrough was private.
But your thriving? **It's public.**
People will look at your life and see evidence of God's faithfulness.

Isaiah 61:3: *"...They will be called oaks of righteousness, a planting of the Lord for the display of his splendor." (NIV).*

Your thriving life becomes a **testimony**.

A mirror of grace.

A signpost of what's possible when someone refuses to quit.

THRIVING IS A DAILY CHOICE

Every day, you get to choose:

- Will I live in fear, or will I move in faith?
- Will I complain, or will I cultivate?
- Will I shrink, or will I show up fully?
- Will I sabotage, or will I step forward?

You won't feel "ready" every day—but the decision to thrive isn't based on feelings. It's based on **truth**.

God says you are chosen.

God says you are equipped.

God says you are free.

God says you are called.

So today—and every day—*choose to thrive.*

YOUR THRIVE SEASON STARTS NOW

You've waited long enough.

You've healed deep wounds.

You've restructured your faith, reclaimed your voice, and restored your joy.

This is your moment to live like the survivor you are and the **warrior you've become**.

Pastor Dr. Claudine Benjamin

You're not who you were.
You're not where you were.
You are rising.
You are radiant.
You are **thriving**.

SCRIPTURES FOR REFLECTION

I am the vine, ye are the branches: He that abideth in me, and I in him, the same bringeth forth much fruit: for without me ye can do nothing. —John 15:5

To appoint unto them that mourn in Zion, to give unto them beauty for ashes, the oil of joy for mourning, the garment of praise for the spirit of heaviness; that they might be called trees of righteousness, the planting of the Lord, that he might be glorified. —Isaiah 61:3

And he shall be like a tree planted by the rivers of water, that bringeth forth his fruit in his season; his leaf also shall not wither; and whatsoever he doeth shall prosper. —Psalm 1:3

He that trusteth in his riches shall fall; but the righteous shall flourish as a branch. —Proverbs 11:28

Blessed is the man that trusteth in the Lord, and whose hope the Lord is. For he shall be as a tree planted by the waters, and that spreadeth out her roots by the river, and shall not see when heat cometh, but her leaf shall be green; and shall not be careful in the year of drought, neither shall cease from yielding fruit. —Jeremiah 17:7–8

Now unto him that is able to do exceeding abundantly above all that we ask or think, according to the power that worketh in us, — Ephesians 3:20

DECLARATION

This is my time to thrive. I let go of fear, guilt, and small thinking. I choose growth, peace, joy, and overflow. I am not afraid to shine. I am not afraid to build. I am not afraid to believe. I walk in power, I live in purpose, and I thrive with boldness. What God has planted in me will bear fruit. I am thriving—in every area of my life.

CONCLUSION

YOU WERE BORN FOR MORE THAN SURVIVAL

Y ou've traveled through pages of truth, layers of healing, and seasons of breakthrough.

You've confronted the pain.
You've silenced the shame.
You've taken the mask off.
You've let go of Egypt.
You've stepped into Canaan.
You've chosen presence.
You've built foundations.
You've reclaimed your dreams.
You've learned to **live again**.

But this is not the end of your journey. It's the beginning of a new chapter. One where you don't just exist or endure—you **flourish**, fully alive, anchored in identity, and unafraid to take up space in the life God destined for you.

YOU ARE THE EVIDENCE OF WHAT GOD CAN DO

You are walking proof that survival doesn't have to be permanent.
You are the story that says healing is possible.
You are the voice that reminds others, "It's okay to hope again."
You are the reflection of redemption in progress.
You are the fruit that bloomed from a storm-soaked seed.

There's a reason the enemy tried to take you out—because he saw your potential.

But you're still here.
And now, you're rising.
You're moving differently.
You're thinking clearer.
You're loving deeper.
You're living **freely**.

THIS IS YOUR PERMISSION SLIP TO LIVE FULLY

You don't need anyone's approval to start enjoying your life.

- You don't have to wait for every area to be perfect.
- You don't have to go back and explain yourself to anyone.
- You don't have to carry guilt for choosing joy.
- You don't have to shrink to make others comfortable.
- You don't have to over-explain why you're doing things differently now.

You've been through enough. Now it's time to walk forward **unapologetically whole.**

HEALING WAS THE PROCESS. LIVING IS THE PROMISE.

You didn't just survive to say you made it. You survived to:

- Live with **purpose.**
- Love without fear.
- Create from peace.
- Lead with wisdom.
- Worship from wholeness.
- Rest without guilt.
- Multiply joy, faith, and impact.

This is your **promised land**.
Not because it's problem-free, but because you're *finally free.*

YOU'RE NOT DONE BECOMING

There will still be valleys. Still be stretching. Still be refining.

But now, you walk in **power**, not panic.
Now, you speak in **faith**, not fear.
Now, you move with **vision**, not just survival instinct.

You'll fall—but now, you know how to get up.
You'll weep—but now, you know joy returns.
You'll question—but now, you know where your help comes from.
And when others see your life, they won't just see you.
They'll see the God who carried you here.

THE REST OF THE STORY IS YOURS TO WRITE

This book may be ending, but your journey is still unfolding.

And now—you get to write it intentionally.

- Start the business.
- Say yes to the trip.
- Launch the ministry.
- Apply to the school.
- Finish the song.
- Embrace the friendship.
- Speak the truth.
- Live without apology.
- Thrive with purpose.

This is not your survival story anymore.
This is your **freedom anthem**.

Sing it loud.
Live it bold.
And never, ever forget—**you were born to live.**

FINAL DECLARATION

I declare that I have mastered survival mode, and I now choose to live. I let go of fear, shame, delay, and scarcity. I embrace the fullness of God's plan for my life. I will walk in joy. I will thrive in purpose. I will love without fear. I will rise without guilt. My life is a reflection of grace, a testimony of strength, and a vessel of glory. I don't just survive—I live. And I live well.

SCRIPTURE INDEX

IDENTITY AND PURPOSE

- Genesis 1:27 – Created in God's image.
- Jeremiah 29:11 – Plans to prosper you.
- Ephesians 2:10 – God's workmanship.
- Isaiah 62:2 – You will be called by a new name.
- Romans 8:28 – All things work together for good.
- 1 Peter 2:9 – A chosen people, a royal priesthood.
- Philippians 1:6 – He will complete the work in you.

HEALING AND WHOLENESS

- Jeremiah 30:17 – I will restore your health.
- Psalm 147:3 – He heals the brokenhearted.
- Luke 17:19 – Your faith has made you whole.
- Isaiah 61:1 – Sent to bind up the brokenhearted.
- Joel 2:25 – I will restore the years the locusts have eaten.
- Psalm 23:3 – He restores my soul.
- Ezekiel 36:26 – I will give you a new heart.

FAITH AND MOVING FORWARD

- Hebrews 11:1 – Faith is the substance of things hoped for.
- James 2:17 – Faith without works is dead.
- Lamentations 3:22–23 – His mercies are new every morning.

- Mark 5:34 – Your faith has healed you.
- Joshua 1:9 – Be strong and courageous.
- Isaiah 43:18–19 – See, I am doing a new thing.
- Psalm 27:13 – I will see the goodness of the Lord.

FREEDOM AND DELIVERANCE

- Deuteronomy 1:6 – You have stayed long enough at this mountain.
- Exodus 16:3 – Looking back at Egypt.
- Joshua 5:9 – Today I have rolled away the reproach.
- John 8:32 – The truth will set you free.
- Galatians 5:1 – It is for freedom that Christ has set us free.

ABUNDANCE AND THRIVING

- John 10:10 – Life to the full.
- Ephesians 3:20 – Immeasurably more than we ask or imagine.
- Proverbs 3:10 – Your barns will be filled.
- Deuteronomy 8:2 – God led you through the wilderness.
- Psalm 1:3 – Like a tree planted by streams of water.
- Jeremiah 17:7–8 – Blessed is the one who trusts in the Lord.
- Proverbs 11:28 – The righteous thrive like a green leaf.

GRATITUDE AND PRESENCE

- 1 Thessalonians 5:18 – Give thanks in all circumstances.
- Psalm 118:24 – This is the day the Lord has made.
- Psalm 100:4 – Enter his gates with thanksgiving.
- Ecclesiastes 3:13 – Satisfaction is the gift of God.
- Philippians 4:11–13 – I have learned to be content.

RELATIONSHIPS AND BOUNDARIES

- Proverbs 4:23 – Guard your heart.
- Amos 3:3 – Can two walk together unless they agree?
- Ecclesiastes 4:9–10 – Two are better than one.
- Matthew 5:37 – Let your yes be yes.
- Galatians 6:5 – Each should carry their own load.
- Matthew 12:50 – Who does the will of my Father is my family.
- 1 Corinthians 13:7 – Love never gives up.

SEASONS, GROWTH, AND WAITING

- Ecclesiastes 3:1 – There is a time for everything.
- Romans 5:3–4 – Suffering produces character and hope.
- Psalm 46:10 – Be still and know.
- Isaiah 40:31 – They will run and not grow weary.
- Galatians 6:9 – Do not become weary in doing good.
- Zechariah 4:10 – Do not despise small beginnings.
- Psalm 138:8 – The Lord will fulfill his purpose for me.